Authors: Ilse Diehl, Markus Hederer

Acrylic Painting
for Beginners

Drawings and paintings: Ilse Diehl, Dagmar Ropertz
Photographs: Markus Hederer

h.f.ullmann

© Tandem Verlag, Königswinter
Original title: *Acrylmalerei für Einsteiger*
ISBN: 978-3-8331-4604-6
All rights reserved

Authors: Ilse Diehl and Markus Hederer, Mainz
Expert advice: Gerd Stegner, Mainz
Paintings, drawings, graphics: Ilse Diehl, Mainz and Dagmar Ropertz, Ober-Olm
Photography: Markus Hederer, Mainz
Editing and production: Markus Hederer, Mainz
Proofreading: Karin Schulze-Langendorff, Hünstetten
Design and production: K.Design, Wiesbaden

© 2008 for the English edition: Tandem Verlag GmbH
h.f.ullmann is an imprint of Tandem Verlag GmbH

Translation: Rae Walter in association with First Edition Translations Ltd, Cambridge, UK
Editing: Lin Thomas in association with First Edition Translations Ltd, Cambridge, UK

Printed in China

ISBN: 978-3-8331-4605-3

10 9 8 7 6 5 4 3 2 1
X X VIII VII VI IV III II I

Contents

Materials

For beginners, one of the advantages of painting with acrylics is that you don't need much in the way of materials. Just a few paints, a brush, a support (the surface to be painted on), and a jar of water, and you're ready to start. The basic equipment is presented on the following pages.

Detailed instructions on the best way to use paints, brushes, and so on will be given in later chapters. It is important to get to know the materials and their characteristics, accessories, and aids in order to be able to achieve all the desired effects.

ACRYLIC PAINTS

Welcome to the colorful world of acrylic paints! You don't know anything about painting yet? Then you've made the right choice with acrylics! They're easy to use, simple and clean to handle, flexible, waterproof, and durable. The best way to learn about their characteristics is by practicing and experimenting. What's more, acrylic paints adhere very well to all kinds of surfaces: fabric, paper, card, fiberboard, wood, and plastic, and to almost any support material or decorative object. You can already see that your imagination can have free rein.

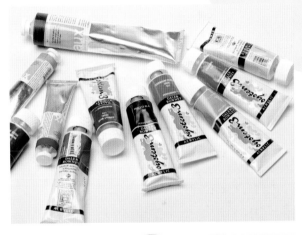

Acrylic paints come in various types of container: tubes, plastic bottles, or plastic tubs. There are also variations in color quality, i.e. the proportion of pigment. There's a distinction between top quality artist's colors and good quality school or studio paints.

SOFT AND HEAVY-BODY

Acrylic paints come not only in different containers and with different pigment contents, they also come in different consistencies. They can be divided into soft-body paints, which usually come in plastic bottles and flow out under light pressure, and what are known as heavy-body paints, which have a consistency similar to butter. These usually come in tubes or, if they are particularly firm, in plastic tubs.

For soft-body paint you usually use a brush, whereas heavy-body paints are often applied with a palette knife. In between these, anything goes, because you can mix all the different consistencies without any problem.

Tip
Note that heavy-body paints take longer to dry. This is important when you want to add the next layer of paint, so you don't get any unwanted mixtures. Also, you should store your painting to dry in such a way that the colors can't run unintentionally.

Soft-body paints are squeezed out of the plastic bottle. Palettes with wells are perfect for holding the paint and preparing it for mixing. They prevent the colors from inadvertently running into one another. Alternatively, you could use yogurt pots, disposable plastic plates or similar.

Scoop heavy-body paints out of the tub with a palette knife and mix either on a palette or directly on the support.

The great advantage of all kinds of acrylic paints is that they can be mixed together—regardless of quality, pigment content, and consistency.

6

ACRYLIC PAINTS FROM PIGMENTS

Pigments are colorants of either organic or inorganic origin. Unlike dyes, pigments are not soluble and therefore need a medium such as oil or acrylic resin. Organic pigments are obtained from plants and animals; inorganic pigments come from earth, minerals, and metals. The pigments we use for painting today are almost exclusively synthetic (artificially produced). Pigments are sold in the form of fine powders, irrespective of their origin or method of production. With the help of some acrylic additive, you can produce your own paints without difficulty. To get you further into the subject of paints, on pages 8 and 9 we will show you the best way to do this.

Plant colors are produced from such things as beets, Japanese blue algae, wild saffron, and stinging nettles. These natural extracts give brilliant colors but they are inclined to fade in the light.

As well as natural pigments there are also synthetic pigments produced by chemical processes. These also include pure white pigments (here titanium white) and effect pigments, which create changing shades of color depending on how the light falls on them.

Various pigments at a glance: three earth pigments on the right, synthetically produced blue, yellow, red, green, and violet pigments, and three plant colors, two of them on the left.

MAKING YOUR OWN ACRYLIC PAINTS

In order to turn the various pigments into usable acrylic paints, you must mix them with a binder in a suitable container and stir them together to make them into paints. For this you will need your chosen pigment, an acrylic binder, mortar and pestle, and possibly a thickener. You should also have either an empty tube or an opaque container with a lid at the ready for storing your paint. A spatula or a miniature dough scraper is the best thing for getting the paint out of the mortar. Now go through the following step by step.

1 Put equal quantities of pigment and acrylic binder in the mortar.

2 Stir to a smooth paste with the pestle.

3 If the paint has become too runny, add more pigment if you want to keep the intensity of the color or add a little thickener. Thickener will make the color more transparent and eventually make a heavy-body paint.

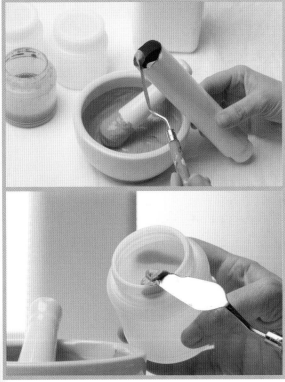

4 Transfer the finished paint to a tube or an opaque container with a lid. Adding a thin layer of water before closing will prevent the paint from drying out.

5 When the tube is full, fold the end over several times. Then you will be able to get the paint out in suitable amounts.

MEDIUMS

Classic mediums are used to change the color in a particular way: thinning it—for example with water—, thickening it and giving it more body, lengthening the drying time with retarders, and many others.

In addition, there are mediums that produce all kinds of effects when mixed with the paint or applied afterward. The paint becomes shinier, rougher, acquires light effects, glimmers and glistens, becomes more transparent or duller, etc. etc. These mediums are called texture gels. They are much used in modern experimental painting, when objects such as threads, strips of paper, and shells are being worked into the painting.

1 Before—after: in this case, a medium that dries transparent and shiny.

2 A smooth texture gel was mixed with the paint, thin layers of orange color, to bring out the structures.

3 Extra rough texture gel. The texture gel was mixed with the paint and applied on top of the paint.

4 Gold sparkle gel was applied on top of the paint.

5 Super-heavy gel paste applied on top of the paint.

Mediums and their effects

Medium	Use/effect
Retarder	Prevents the paint from drying too quickly and makes it possible to work longer with the current color. This makes it easier to create color flows.
Thickener	Gives body to fluid paints to give thicker cover.
Transparent medium, drying shiny	The medium is mixed with the paint. The color becomes shinier.
Heavy medium, drying white	The medium is mixed with the paint. The color becomes shinier.
Dull drying medium	The medium is mixed with the paint. The color becomes duller.
Smooth texture gel	Thick, heavy application, surface smooth to shiny, can be modeled.
Rough texture gel	Thick, heavy application, surface rough, can be modeled.
Extra-rough texture gel	Thick, heavy application, surface very rough, can be modeled.
Gel with gold sparkles	Thick, lightweight application, surface shiny and glittery.
Gel with hologram glitter	Thick, lightweight application, surface shiny and glittery.
Shiny varnish	Smooth application with brush, shiny paint surface.
Extra-heavy gel	Thick, lightweight application, paint surface shiny with structure.

BRUSHES, PAINTING KNIVES ETC.

Painting starts when paint is applied to a ground. In acrylic painting, various implements are used for this purpose. First and foremost among them is, of course, the brush, the classic artist's tool. But that is not enough. The different paint consistencies alone make it sensible and necessary to have other equipment. This includes a great variety of knives and all kinds of sponges, even items of window-cleaning equipment, if it's a question of experimentation—not to mention your own ten fingers, which are of course perfect for applying paint.

There is a wide range of tools for use in applying acrylic paint. Alongside the classic brush, we have palette knives, sponges, and even household items.

BRUSHES FOR COVERING LARGE SURFACES

Basically there are three occasions for using brushes with which you can quickly cover a large surface with paint.

1. An initial application for laying out a picture (page 35 ff.)
2. Applying a toned ground (imprimatura)
3. Experimental and expressionist painting.

The brushes used for covering large surfaces are either very broad or thick and round with many bristles.

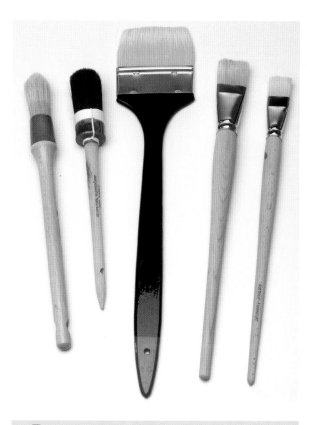

BRUSHES FOR ORDINARY PAINTING

In this case, almost exclusively flat brushes are used. The bristles are either natural hair or, especially for acrylic painting, made of artificial fibers such as nylon or perlon. Either way a long handle is important, because a long lever helps you to get the right sweep. It also makes it easier to keep a suitable distance from the support. These brushes can be used to apply all paints, of all consistencies.

Medium sized, flat brushes with long handles can be used for all purposes and are the tools most commonly used.

FINE BRUSHES

Fine round brushes are particularly important for the finish—the final application—highlights, fine lines, branches and lots more. And even though, as a beginner, you probably shouldn't be thinking of it, there is no better tool for signing your paintings.

The paintbrush is one of the earliest human inventions—not only for artistic expression but also more particularly as a tool for craftsmen.

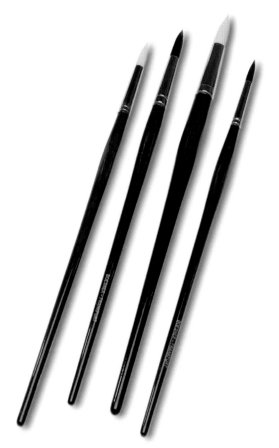

Fine brushes are usually round and have an elegantly tapering point.

You should get yourself a selection of the available types of paintbrushes. This absolutely must include flat brushes sizes 20, 16, 12, 10, 8, and 6, round brushes sizes 20 and 8, and a "coarser" one (left).

PROTECTION FOR BRUSHES

Make sure when buying a round brush that it has a plastic sheath that you can put over the head of the brush after drying. This will help to keep its shape so you will get lasting pleasure from this valuable tool.

The regular use of the protector that comes with your round brush will keep it in shape.

> ### *Advice*
> *Always take care to clean your brushes thoroughly after use with water and maybe a little soap or brush cleaner, and restore the hairs to the original shape with your fingers.*

Lay the brushes flat to dry so water doesn't penetrate the handle.

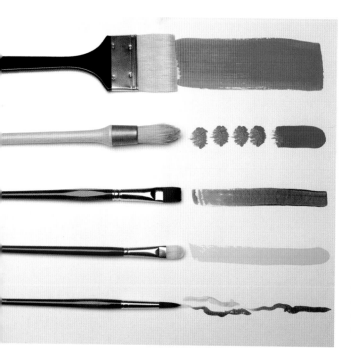

TRYING OUT BRUSHES

To familiarize yourself with paints and brushes, you should try out both in various combinations. Start by using a simple acrylic painting block as a ground. That way you will learn how what amount of paint works with which brush and what options you have, for instance if you don't just draw a line with a brush but also dab sometimes. This will soon give you a good idea of all the different ways each brush can be used.

Try out all the different brush shapes. The choice of color doesn't matter to start with. But be sure to vary the amount of water you mix with the paint, so you get to know the effect of different paint consistencies.

PAINTING KNIVES

Alongside brushes, knives are the tools most often used for applying paint. There are even some artists who prefer to use knives and don't use brushes at all.

Painting knives come in a number of different versions. Plastic or rubber knives are widely used for painting with acrylics, as well as traditional palette knives with metal blades and wooden handles. If buying the latter, go for good quality knives that will not rust.

Knives are especially good for applying structure pastes and heavy-body paints. They make it possible to create particularly attractive special effects.

Painting knives at a glance: one model in rubber, three in yellow plastic, and a whole variety in metal with wooden handles.

Sponges have a wide variety of uses—including painting, and even a humble sponge scouring pad can be used for more than just cleaning pans.

SPONGES

You can use sponges for applying paint to a large area, deliberately smudging paint in order to achieve an intentional effect, and for dabbing on various designs.

All kinds of natural and household sponges can be used.

TRYING OUT KNIVES AND SPONGES

To familiarize yourself with painting knives and sponges, do the same as you did with brushes and paints. Use various different knives to apply different amounts of heavy-body paints to a simple acrylic painting block, and use a sponge to apply all kinds of ordinary acrylic paint as well.

While knives are good for applying large quantities of strong colors, sponges produce rather more delicate effects.

SUPPORTS

Acrylics can be used to paint on so many different surfaces that you can use almost anything you fancy as a support. A "support" simply means the surface you paint on. In fact, any surface can be a support, a fate regrettably suffered by many walls. Beginners in acrylic painting will naturally be attracted at first to conventional supports. These include:
- Acrylic painting blocks,
- Artist's boards
- Stretched canvases
- Wood.

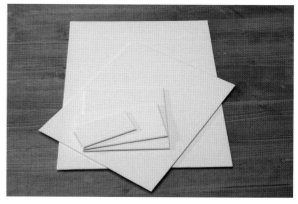

Artist's boards are usually laminated with cotton fabric and are already primed. You can work directly onto the surface and also stand them on an easel. They come in a wide range of shapes and sizes.

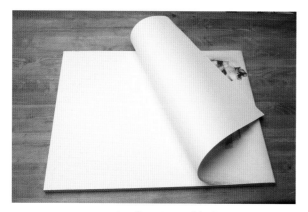

Acrylic painting blocks are distinguished by the use of very thick paper that hardly wrinkles even when very wet. The sheets are glued together so they can't blow away, but when your painting has dried, it can be easily detached from the block.

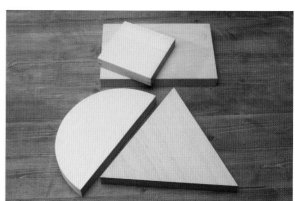

Wood is one of the oldest, most traditional supports. Now available in new, more attractive shapes, wood has been enjoying something of a renaissance as a support for painting. Triangular, semicircular, rectangular, and square blocks are pretty and look expensive.

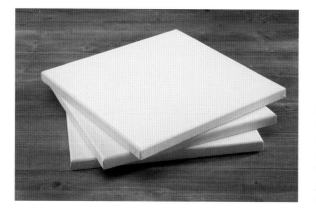

Stretched canvases are among the most popular supports. There is an incomparable range of shapes and sizes, and their great advantage is that, when you have finished, you can hang your work directly with no need for a frame.

PRIMING WOOD

Whatever the support, be it canvas, cotton or wood, it is important to prime it before starting to paint. This prevents the support from absorbing too much paint and making work unnecessarily difficult for you. In addition, a light-colored base coat increases the luminescence of the colors and thus has a positive influence on the overall effect of the picture. A good base coat also makes the piece more durable.

We use a wooden support to show you how to apply a coat of primer. For acrylic paintings, use a white emulsion paint (often called acrylic gesso) for the outer surface. Apply the paint in two thin, even coats, using a broad, flat brush. Make sure the first coat has dried before applying the second.

Tip
For a particularly fine primer coat, when the first coat has dried, rub it with fine sandpaper, apply the second coat, and rub down again when this has dried.

To prime wood *apply two thin, even coats of white emulsion.*

Advice
You don't have a palette or a disposable plate to hand? No problem: cover an ordinary plate with aluminum foil and mix your paints on that. The good thing about this is that, at the end of the session, you let the remains of the paint dry and throw them out with the foil.

A plate, *a piece of aluminum foil, and your palette is ready to use!*

PALETTES

Before applying paint to the support, it is often advisable to mix them first in order to achieve the desired shade. For this purpose, artists and craftsmen have for centuries used a palette—a plate on which they can do just that. Nowadays you can find all sorts of palettes, but it is definitely an advantage if it is the same color as the support. In most cases, that means a white palette. In addition, it is useful to have a palette with wells for acrylics, so you can work safely with paints that may be runny.

A plastic palette with wells *is best for fluid paints. Heavy-body paints can be mixed on disposable palettes. Disposable plates covered with cellophane make a cheap alternative.*

SCALING AIDS

If you want to copy a picture as a subject for your painting, you can use a grid to transfer the contours to your support with the correct proportions. This process is described in detail on pages 28 and 29. The equipment you need consists of a sheet of paper, a ruler or tape measure, string, scissors, and masking tape.

Scaling aids
at a glance.

EASELS

An easel makes it easier to work on a picture. You can set it to the height and angle that best suits your method of working at any time. This means you can virtually eliminate problems caused by too great a difference between the level of the picture and that of the subject.

Easels come in many different sizes and price ranges. When buying, be guided mainly by the size of the support on which you want to paint. A second important aspect is maximum stability. To guarantee this, you should not hesitate to buy the best you can afford.

Wooden easel
that will safely take pictures
up to 47 inches (1.20 m).

STAY CLEAN!

Acrylic paint dries quickly—often too quickly! A spot on the carpet, your best skirt or new sweater will not come out once it has dried. So there's only one thing for it: prevention! Protect yourself, your clothing, and your rooms from spots of paint by covering your workspace and wearing working clothes rather than anything smart. Fresh spots on smooth surfaces can be wiped off quickly with paper towels. On fabrics, the only thing that helps is to wash them out quickly.

Small ways to combat big spots: working clothes, protective film, and paper towels.

Color theory

The number of different colors seems to be infinite, yet all bright colors are based on the three primary colors yellow, cyan, and magenta. When two of these are mixed together, a secondary color is produced. However, if you really want to be able to produce all colors, you also need the achromatic (or neutral) colors black and white. If you experiment you will find out which mixtures produce which colors and be able to create your own palette.

THE PRIMARY COLORS

The three primary colors are yellow, cyan, and magenta. They are distinguished by being absolutely pure. This means that yellow contains only yellow and no trace of any other color. This is also true of cyan, a pure blue, and for magenta, which is a pure shade of red. By mixing them in the appropriate proportions, you can theoretically produce all other chromatic colors.

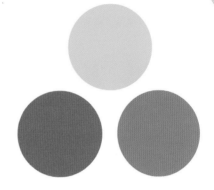

The three primary colors: yellow, cyan, and magenta.

THE SECONDARY COLORS

Secondary colors are made by mixing two primary colors in the proportion of 50:50. Yellow and cyan make green, yellow and magenta a reddish orange, and cyan and magenta mix to produce violet. If you alter the proportions in the mixture, the shades of the secondary color will also be altered. So with secondary colors you can already cover a broad spectrum of different colors. To try this out and get a good grasp of color mixes, you should treat yourself to paints in the primary colors and combine them to your heart's content.

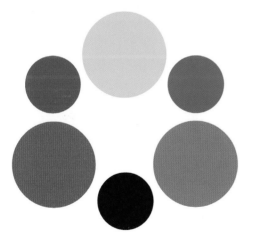

The mixing of each pairing of primary colors produces a secondary color. Yellow and cyan give green, yellow and magenta make an orange-red, and cyan and magenta produce violet-blue.

Try making different shades of secondary colors to get a feel for color mixing.

COMPLEMENTARY COLORS

There is one more important term in color theory: complementary colors. On a color wheel of primary and secondary colors, the secondary color lying opposite a primary color is its complementary color. This means that the secondary color green is the complementary color of the primary color magenta, orange-red is the complementary color of cyan, and violet-blue is the complementary color of yellow.

This knowledge, which may at first seem purely theoretical, is in practice much used in painting. The reason is that, when it's a question of making colors look bright and/or achieve maximum contrast, applying two complementary colors next to one another is a tried and tested method. This is not only true of primary colors and secondary colors that are a precise 50:50 mix, it also works for all the shades on the color wheel. You find the complementary color of any color by drawing a straight line from it through the center of the circle to the opposite side.

One more thing: if you mix two complementary colors together, the result is warm tones of brown and gray.

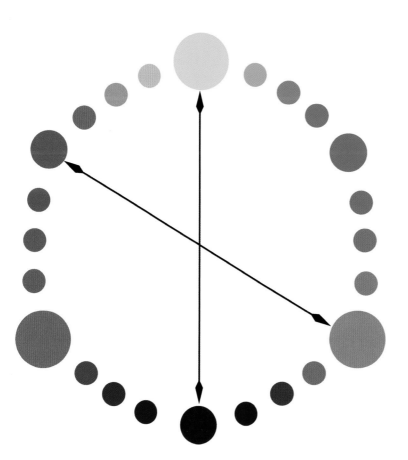

Tip
When looking for a complementary color, you can also be successful if you paint a large enough area of paper, hold the result up in front of a white wall, and stare at it for about two minutes. If you then remove the paper and look at the white background wall, you will see the complementary color you are looking for.

A color wheel with the primary colors yellow, cyan, and magenta, plus the secondary and complementary colors. If you mix two primary colors, the result is always the complementary color of the third primary color. Also, you can find the complementary color of a complementary color by drawing a straight line from it through the center of the circle to the opposite side.

Colors are especially bright and effective when they are applied next to their complementary colors. For example, orange-red appears most intense when surrounded by cyan blue.

THE MOST IMPORTANT COLORS FOR ACRYLIC PAINTING

To be honest, there are probably no painters who mix all their colors just from the three primary colors and the achromatic colors black and white. It simply would not be practical, especially as there are countless paints available from which you can easily mix the most frequently used shades.

Using ready-made acrylic paints also has the advantage that, if you particularly like bright colors, you can instantly get hold of, say, a strong orange that might easily look a little dirty if you had mixed it yourself. You will soon see that, after a few attempts, you will "home in" on a selection of colors from which you will create your personal palette. For beginners, we suggest a basic set of colors for acrylic painting.

One more thing to note: the three primary colors yellow, cyan, and magenta, as presented in color theory, come from the world of computing and in practice they are not nearly so widespread in painting. As primary colors for your own acrylic painting, it would be better to use cadmium yellow light or chrome yellow, ultramarine, and vermilion. Their brightness remains unsurpassed.

COLOR NAMES

The colors shown here, which can of course be bought, constitute a recommended basic kit for acrylic painting. These are:

- **Titanium white**
- **Cadmium yellow light**
- **Vermilion**
- **Dark madder**
- **Ultramarine**
- **Prussian blue**
- **Chromium oxide green fiery**
- **Umber**
- **Burnt Sienna**
- **Light ocher**
- **Black**

21

CREATING A COLOR-MIXING GRID

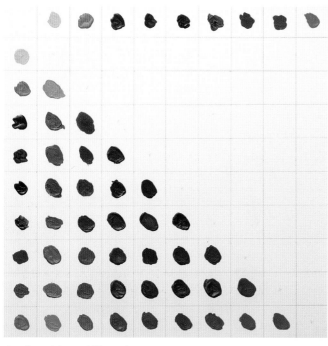

As a first exercise in color mixing, draw a regular grid on an acrylic block and apply your eleven colors, each in its own square, horizontally along the top edge and vertically down the left side. Then, working downward, mix each of the colors in the top row about 50:50 with those from the left row, either on a palette or on a plate covered with aluminum foil, preferably with a paintbrush. Transfer the result to the appropriate "intersection field," which will give you a collection of mixed colors in the form of a triangle—your first color mixing grid. It will show you what shades it is possible to create by mixing the paints in your basic kit.

A color-mixing grid from the paints in the basic kit. Mix your own personal color grid from your paints.

MIXING SHADES

Mixing paints in the proportion 50:50 is only one possibility. You can produce many more shades by mixing two colors in different proportions. Take, for instance, vermilion and ultramarine. As you add more blue to the mixture, the shade changes from the violet of the 50:50 mixture to an increasingly strong violet-blue. The greater the proportion of red, the more the shade changes to a reddish purple. Try mixing shades with all paints in various combinations to make all kinds of different things happen!

Mixing cadmium yellow and ultramarine. In seven stages, more and more blue was added to the yellow on the left. The far right field is 100 percent ultramarine.

LIGHTER AND DARKER TONES

In addition to the mixing of two bright colors, lightening with white and darkening with black are two other important methods when it comes to producing intentional mixtures of paint. Start in the same way by creating various color grids.

This is how it works: Apply a color in the middle of the scale. To lighten, add more and more white. The tone will become lighter until it reaches white. You darken the color by adding black. The tone becomes darker until it reaches black.

So you see, by mixing shades of color and lightening or darkening them you can create an enormous range of every color imaginable and give free rein to your imagination.

> ### Advice
> **Warm and cold colors can have an enormous influence on the mood of a picture. This plays a particularly important part in landscape painting.**

Lightening and darkening vermilion: *The color at the center of the scale was mixed with more and more white on the left, and more and more black on the right.*

WARM COLORS

The warm colors include all red tones through orange to yellow and through reddish violet and brown to ocher. They are mixed from all the red and yellow colors on the color wheel. To tone down warm colors, blue from among the cold shades can be mixed with them. Lightening and darkening play an equally significant role.

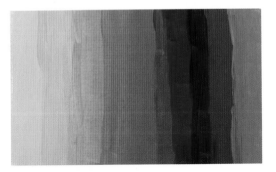

Warm colors, *set beside one another and mixed from the eleven acrylic paints recommended on page 21.*

COLD COLORS

The cold colors include all shades of blue, through turquoise to green. They are mixed from all the blue and yellow shades on the color wheel. To brighten cold colors, red from among the warm shades can be mixed with them. For instance, a cold violet can result from the right mixture of blue and red. As with the warm colors, lightening and darkening help to increase the selection of colors.

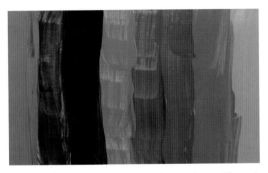

Cold colors, *set beside one another and mixed from the eleven acrylic paints recommended for beginners on page 21.*

COLOR EFFECTS AND MEANINGS

As well as the various effects colors may have, they have always conveyed a wide variety of meanings. As a rule, the colors used by an artist flow perfectly into the picture without further assistance. On the other hand, it can be an advantage to know the qualities attributed to a color and use them intentionally from time to time. With this in mind, we will now present the major colors and the properties that are generally associated with them.

Blue *is cool. It's the color of the sky and the sea and conveys calm, trust, peace, dutifulness, beauty, and longing. However, blue also stands for dreaminess, coldness, neglectfulness, and melancholy.*

Yellow *is the color of the sun. It conveys light, happiness, and joy, and stands for knowledge, wisdom, reason, and logic. Dirty yellow tones have negative associations such as illness, deception, vindictiveness, ambition, danger, pessimism, egoism, miserliness, and envy.*

Violet *is a dignified color. It is associated with inspiration, magic, mysticism, and art. It is considered unusual and flamboyant and is also associated with piety, penitence, and self-sacrifice. The negative effects of violet are pride, arrogance, and immorality.*

Green *is the color of vegetation, of woods and meadows. Green is calming and stands for generosity, reliability, harmony, normality, hope, and the renewal of life.*
However, it also has negative connotations such as envy, indifference, stagnation, and tiredness.

Cyan, *also known as turquoise, is the fresh color of the sea on a sunny day. It is associated with alertness, consciousness, spiritual openness, and clarity. On the other hand, cyan can seem very cool and distant and evoke a feeling of emptiness.*

White as ice and snow...purity, clarity, innocence, and solemnity are associated with white, as well as peace, ease, and cleanliness.
On the other hand, white is also unapproachable; it stands for cool reserve, vulnerability, sterility, and capitulation.

Magenta is gentle and means idealism, gratitude, involvement, order, and sympathy.
However, snobbishness, arrogance, and dominance are also linked to magenta.

Red is the color of fire. It arouses attention, is full of energy and vitality, and stands for love, passion, and sexuality. Red is aggressive and agitating. It means anger, rage, brutality, blood, war and, not least, the color of the devil.

Gray is a cloudy sky on a gloomy day. Perfect neutrality, caution, restraint, willingness to compromise, dignity, and devotion are closely associated with gray.
Gray is not very striking and may appear boring and monotonous. Uncertainty and depression are gray, as are bewilderment and decay.

Orange is the color of sunsets and symbolizes optimism and a zest for life. It is a sign of open-mindedness, sociability, youthfulness, health, and self-confidence.
Orange also conveys irresponsibility, obtrusiveness, and dissipation.

Black is dark, without light, the color of night.
It means sorrow, impenetrability, immutability, fear, and secrecy, as well as anxiety, emptiness, seclusion, and death.
However, black can also appear dignified and stands for respect and ceremony.

LOCAL AND APPARENT COLOR

Local color can be defined as a pure-toned color—uninfluenced by light and shade and without the addition of black or white. It also means the true color of an object. A tomato is red, a banana is yellow, the sky is blue, a leaf is green, an orange is orange, and so on. That's how children, for example, paint their pictures, giving everyday objects their typical colors.

By contrast, local color plays a subordinate role in naturalistic painting. Here what is known as apparent color—the color that the artist perceives an object, a figure, or a part of the landscape to be—is much more important. It depends very much on the conditions, particularly the way the light falls and how it is reflected. The picture of a stream (below left) illustrates the various apparent colors of the water.

Apparent colors are also influenced by their immediate surroundings. If, for example, a banana is lying next to a tomato, the reflection of its yellow color will cause part of the tomato to appear orange, while the reflection of the red color will turn parts of the banana orange. In this case, the apparent color is influenced by a reflection color.

APPLYING PAINT

We are now returning slowly but surely from theory to practice. Back on page 6, we presented paints of different consistencies—soft and heavy-body. These different consistencies make it possible to apply paint in a variety of ways, enabling you to achieve many interesting and attractive effects.

Application can be divided into
• Impasto (thick)
• Opaque (flat)
• Glazing (transparent).

Impasto appears thicker and cruder, and makes it easier to work objects into the surface. Applying the paint flat and opaque is probably the most frequently used technique and is very similar to traditional oil painting. Glazing is very delicate and is similar to watercolor technique, but has the advantage that the paints don't fade so readily and, most importantly, they don't smear when wiped.

In practice impasto painting is most often done with a knife, but it is also possible to use a brush. Opaque colors are usually applied with a brush, but you can use a knife. For glazing, a brush or a sponge is recommended.

Various apparent colors of the water in a stream, depending on the way the light falls and how it is reflected. On the left, the apparent colors are picked out again.

Different types of application in vermilion: impasto, opaque, and transparent.

Ideas and subjects

You want to paint, and subjects are as plentiful as sand on the seashore, only…which ones are right for you and what best suits the way you go about things? It's very important to keep your eyes open and collect everything you see that interests you and looks like a suitable subject for a painting. It might be examples of other paintings, but it could also be a stone or a shell picked up on the beach that you later paint, or attach to the picture using thick impasto, or draw inspiration from in some other way.

FINDING MOTIFS

The word motif is related to the idea of motivation, something that gets you going. So a motif is always something that motivates you to paint a picture, something that attracts and inspires you. The obvious reason for painting is surely to depict something you yourself like, and something you can handle in an artistic manner.

When searching for suitable subjects for your paintings, you will soon strike it lucky if you leaf through books—such as coffee-table books—look at your own photos, rummage through postcards, gaze at posters, or simply wander through the countryside or a picturesque town.

Tip
Start an "ideas collection," in which you gradually store everything you come across. You can also start a folder or a file to hold notes, photos, sketches, press-cuttings, and much more.

*You can find **many** good ideas for your pictures in your immediate surroundings. Books, postcards, or your own photos will provide masses of material.*

TWO-DIMENSIONAL, THREE-DIMENSIONAL

Painting a picture usually means setting it out on a flat surface, and as a rule, the result is two-dimensional. The obvious conclusion is that copying two-dimensional originals is the most appropriate thing for beginners. So before you set about trying to capture complicated spatial (three-dimensional) arrangements on canvas, it would be better to start with two-dimensional models: pictures from books, photos, postcards etc., as described on the previous page. However, because the original you are copying will rarely be the same size as your canvas, you need a way of keeping the proportions correct when transferring the content of the picture. Over the centuries the grid has proved to be the ideal method for this purpose.

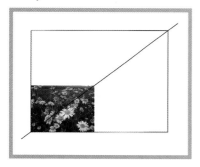

Use a grid to transfer the original onto the support in the correct proportions.

GRIDS

There are two stages to the grid method for transferring the contents of a picture:
1. Checking your selected original to see if it can be enlarged directly to fit the support you have available. This is the case if the diagonal of the support has the same slope as that of the original. However, it may happen that the diagonal of the original has a steeper or shallower gradient than that of the support. In either case, you can adjust them by adding to or subtracting material from the original.

Example 1

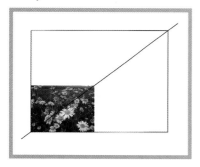

The diagonals of the original and the support are identical, so you can transfer the picture directly.

Example 2

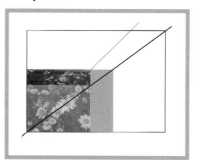

The diagonal of the original is steeper. You can adjust to match either by leaving out parts of the original to reduce the height or by adding subject matter to the width.

Example 3

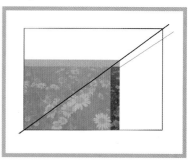

The diagonal of the original is shallower. You can adjust to match either by leaving out parts of the original to reduce the width or by adding subject matter to the height.

2. Once the proportions of the original and the support match, you create grids on the original and the support in the same proportions. Then you transfer the content of each square of the original to the corresponding square on the support, and thus keep the contents in the correct proportions.

Now we will show you step by step how you can transfer an original, in this case a photo, to the support, with the help of scissors, string (thread), ruler, pencil, and masking tape.

1 To check whether your chosen section of the original will—when enlarged in proportion—fit the support, stretch a thread diagonally from the top right to the bottom left of the support.
Fix the thread at the corners with a little masking tape.

2 Now place your original in the bottom left hand corner of the support so the edges match. In this case, the original is not high enough, so it must be extended by adding to the upper and lower parts of the design. With a ruler, measure the distance from the lower edge of the picture to the appropriate place on the diagonal of the support. This measurement corresponds to the height of the extended original. The breadth of the original is already known.

3 Transfer the measurements of the extended original to a piece of paper and cut out.
Stick your original to the paper, then sketch in a few lines extending the design.

4 Now stick the extended original to a bigger piece of paper. Divide the length and breadth evenly into sections (e.g. divide 8 inches (20 cm) into 4 x 2 inch (5 cm)

sections = divide by 4) and mark with a pencil. To divide into squares, stretch threads across it vertically and horizontally, and fix with masking tape.

5 Divide the breadth and height of your support into the same number of squares as your extended original and mark the points with a pencil.

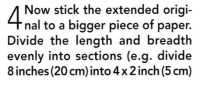

6 To divide into squares, stretch threads across it vertically and horizontally, and fix with masking tape.

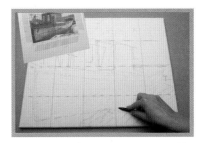

7 Now transfer the content of each square of the original proportionally to the corresponding square on the support. This will create a preliminary sketch.

SKETCHES

Painting directly from a three-dimensional model almost from life is pretty difficult. And anyway, who always has their painting materials with them just when an interesting subject crops up? That's when it can help to have a sketch of something you later want to paint captured with a few quick strokes on a sketchpad. Also, this is a way to make a three-dimensional object into a two-dimensional pattern that will be easier for you to turn into a picture, for reasons already discussed.

Scene in a weekly market in a small turkish town. The two men are deep in conversation as they wait for customers. In this pencil sketch, the goods for sale were also captured in some detail. Market parasols in the background, a few stalls, and hints of people complete the sketch.

This is an architectural sketch, in this case a station in a large city in Germany. It was made on waste paper, which had previously been given a coat of acrylic paint. It was done in felt pen, and quickly captured the structure of the building, the movement of the people hurrying by, and the tranquil elements.

This sketch consists of three cut flowers from a florist, and a glass vase filled with water. The various elements were sketched in charcoal on drawing paper. Attention was paid to how the light falls from the top right, to try to achieve a three-dimensional effect in the painting that was later elaborated from it.

Categories and subjects

There are many reasons for painting pictures, and even more subjects. But because people crave order—especially in the case of art historians—they have naturally grouped different types of painting into a kind of filing system. This has produced what could be described as two filing cabinets with various drawers: cabinet 1—the category or genre, with drawers such as landscape, still life, and architecture; cabinet 2—the subject matter, with drawers such as mythology, nature or politics.

CLASSIFYING A PICTURE

The answer to the question "What does the picture show?" is one of the most important criteria for classifying pictures. It is a question of the subject of the picture.

Well-known and important genres are landscapes, figures, plants, animals, still life, and architecture. However, in each of these drawers there are a few, let's call them record cards, each of which contains a further subdivision. Taking plants as an example, we could mention "botanical studies," "flower pieces," "gardens," and "vegetables."

Ideally a picture can be clearly categorized, but quite often the boundaries are fluid, for example when animals are moving through a beautiful landscape.

You will learn more about individual genres and their subgroups from page 45 on.

Elephants on the move through a breathtaking African landscape. In this picture the boundaries between animal and landscape painting are blurred.

Advice

Filing systems are there to provide an overview and help you to find your way around, but for the painter and his creativity they are not in any way binding. So there is no need to "paint yourself into" a category or decide on one too quickly. Remain versatile until you have found your own style.

This tulip clearly belongs in the "plants" category and is a subject from the subcategory "flower pieces."

Figure painting is a particular challenge for every painter. It's about understanding the proportions of the human body and depicting them correctly—one of the more difficult tasks.

A simple still life, composed of the elements plate and fruits. Composition plays a special part in still life painting, so for beginners it's best to have just a few elements.

Beautiful areas such as these are to be found in southwest Ireland. Landscape is one of the most popular subjects in painting—possibly an expression of man's close attachment to nature.

The categories "architecture" and "landscape" in one picture. La Roque Gageac is one of those villages in southwest France, strung out along the Dordogne in an exciting river landscape that can literally be described as picturesque.

SUBJECT MATTER

A second important way of classifying pictures is division according to subject matter or the answer to the question "What does the picture express?" Typical subjects in painting are religion, war, social matters, mythology, history, sport, technology, nature, the arts, science, and politics. Anyone who paints a picture on a recognizable theme will generally have a message to convey. In most cases this is done through the subject of the painting.

There is no doubt that classification by type is more helpful to the beginner than classification by subject. It requires a certain degree of skill to get to the heart of the meaning of a subject, but you will soon get the idea.

Fun with colors

On the foregoing pages we showed you some typical subjects, but before you start restricting yourself to specific categories, we'd like to suggest a slightly different way of getting into acrylic painting. We turn our backs on the representational and allow color to create its own effects. So don't be afraid of the blank, white canvas—you have color at hand! Apply generously with brush, sponge, and palette knife, and you can easily produce attractive and decorative paintings. And you will be in very good company!

TIME TO START PAINTING

At last it's time to start painting. But don't rush into it headlong. Prepare your workplace carefully beforehand. Protect the table and floor from paint-splashes. Wear comfortable clothing that you're not intending to wear anywhere smart again, so it won't matter if it gets splashed. Then get together the materials you want to use. These must include paints, brushes, palette, a jar of water, and a rag for wiping the brushes. A roll of paper towels will also come in very handy. Depending on whether you're going to paint on an easel or on the table, place your chosen support on it.

Perfectly prepared: paints, brushes, palette, a jar of water, and—last but not least, a rag.

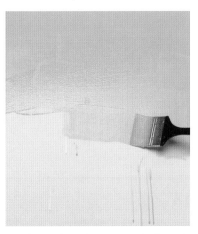

Applying the color energetically with a broad brush and cadmium yellow mixed with a little water.

PLENTY OF PAINT ON A LARGE AREA

There's no reason to sit brooding over a white canvas. Take your first steps in acrylic painting by covering large areas with generous quantities of paint. Take one of your favorite colors, possibly thinned with a little water, and a broad, flat brush—and start covering the canvas with the shade of your choice.

Work with big sweeping movements. It makes you feel good, because you don't have to bother about shapes or other details—and it also gives you quite a feel for the materials you're dealing with. You'll see: in no time at all, the canvas will be covered with paint and the first picture will basically be finished.

A picture in yellow – *finished, even at this stage.*

COMBINING COLORS

A liberal covering of paint doesn't have to be limited to one color. It is fine to use two or three colors that go well with one another and combine them together with relish.

You don't always have to use a brush either. From your generous selection of tools, you can take a household sponge, mix the paints beforehand, and then boldly go ahead. Spread the colors over the canvas one after the other, perhaps in the form of a wave, until all the white areas are covered.

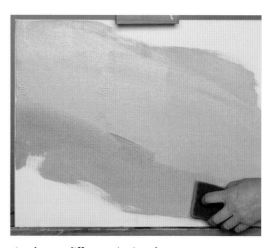

Apply two different *shades of blue to the canvas with a household sponge.*

Squares and rectangles in toning colors *make an effective contrast to the bold sweep of color in the background.*

ADDING ACCENTS

Every picture may be finished at every stage of its creation, but that shouldn't prevent anyone from adding attractive accents. Why not use shapes and colors to add contrast to an extensive area of paint? Hard-edged geometric shapes make an effective contrast to round off the sweeping curves of the first coat of color. This can be achieved by covering parts of the surface with masking tape that will be pulled off later after the paint has been applied.

So be brave and apply plenty of paint to a large area, give your imagination free rein, and create an attractive picture with a personal touch with relatively little effort.

Color without form

In the first picture we paint, we are not interested in specific shapes but in the liberal application of paint to large areas. The basis is a covering coat laid on with a broad brush. After that, a second and third color are dabbed on and smeared with a sponge. There is no need for a preparatory drawing to lay out the composition. Structures created by dabbing and smearing are only partly planned.

Materials

Stretched canvas 24 x 28 inches (60 x 70 cm); flat brush no. 80; natural sponge; jar of water; cotton cloth or paper towels; palette; colors: cadmium yellow light, light ocher, and vermilion

1 Put cadmium yellow onto your palette, dip the brush in water, and thin down the paint a little. Begin applying paint from top to bottom. It should start by being quite thin and be put on in several coats.

 Cadmium yellow light

 Light ocher

 Vermilion

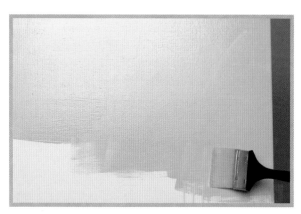

2 Use swift, sweeping, energetic brush strokes to be sure you apply the paint evenly. Take care to cover the canvas completely with paint.

3 Allow the first coat to dry, then add a second and third as required. The end result should be a rich, even shade of color.

4 On your palette, mix a little light ocher into the cadmium yellow and add enough water to make the paint quite runny. Dip a moistened natural sponge in the paint and dab it on the canvas.

5 By dabbing the canvas from the bottom (with more paint) to the top (with slightly less), you will have created a progression. Leave the result to dry.

Tip
Don't completely fill the brush with paint; take it up gradually in smaller portions. This will assure even application.

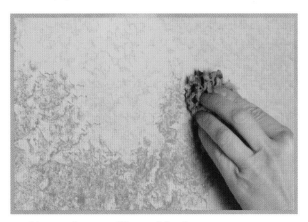

6 Now mix vermilion with the light ocher and cadmium yellow. Don't add any more water. The new color will be slightly less runny. Dip a moistened natural sponge in it and dab it on the canvas.

Tip

After smearing, always take a couple of steps back to consider the result and get fresh inspiration.

7 Now use the sponge to smear the wet paint in places of your choice to give a pattern to the whole picture and create extra effects.

8 Work with greater freedom and energy in the upper parts of the painting.

9 The lighter patches in the center of the picture were created by first washing out the sponge and squeezing it out before smearing. This technique can be used to remove paint from selected areas. The end result is an expressive and dynamic picture created from three colors.

SUMMARY

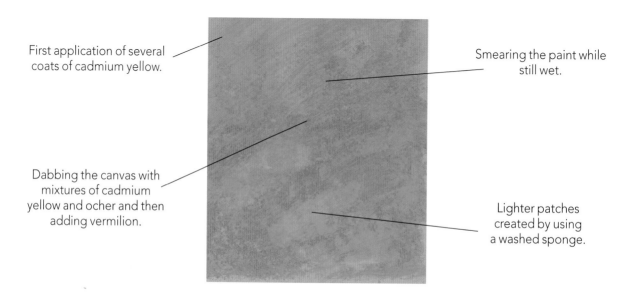

First application of several coats of cadmium yellow.

Smearing the paint while still wet.

Dabbing the canvas with mixtures of cadmium yellow and ocher and then adding vermilion.

Lighter patches created by using a washed sponge.

A picture in red

Rich, cheerful colors also dominate our second picture which, like "color without form," contains no specific objects. But unlike the first painting, here the second covering coat is given a structure by means of the brush marks. Horizontals and verticals determine the directions.

Applying a darker red and painting over it produces interesting figures, or more precisely "color solids."

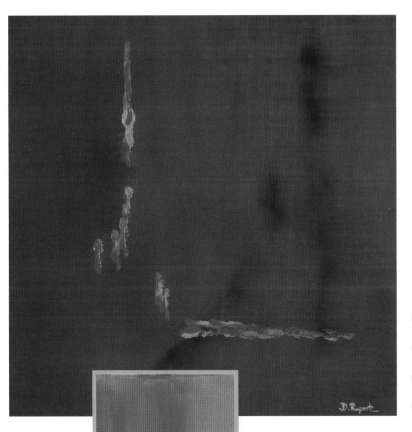

Materials
Stretched canvas 20 x 20 inches (50 x 50 cm); flat brushes nos. 80, 12; jar of water; cotton cloth or paper towels; palette; colors: vermilion, crimson, dark madder, and chrome yellow

Vermilion

Crimson

Dark madder

Chrome yellow

1 Put vermilion on your palette, dip your brush in the water, and thin the paint a little with it. Start applying paint from top to bottom. It should be fairly thin to begin with.

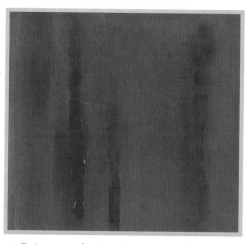

2 The second coat of vermilion applied with the size 80 flat brush should cover completely. Lines resulting from the brush strokes are totally intentional.

3 Paint streaks in crimson in a few places, using a narrower brush and much thicker paint.

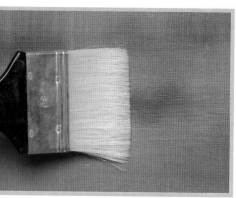

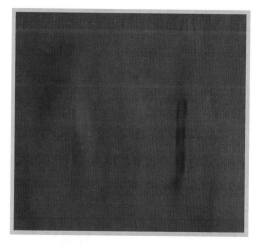

4 Then paint over these places again with the broad brush both horizontally and vertically. Depending on the direction of the brush strokes, blurred figures will appear, which can also be described as "color solids."

5 Break up the crimson by overpainting with madder, which is darker. Brighten lighter patches by applying more vermilion.

6 Now paint over these places again with the broad flat brush vertically, horizontally, and also diagonally in order to achieve even more attractive effects.

Tip

Starting no later than with the second coat, work "wet into wet"—so avoid letting the paints dry before starting the next application.

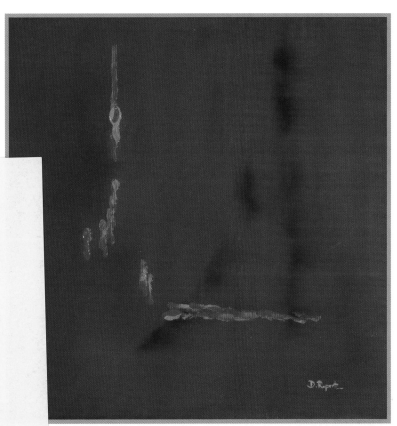

...contrasts in the painting are created by the various colors, their ...rent tonal values, and also the direction (horizontal, vertical, or ...l) and the way in which the paint was applied. Dark colors retreat ...background, while bright colors are more striking. The very thick ...also heightens the effect.

SUMMARY

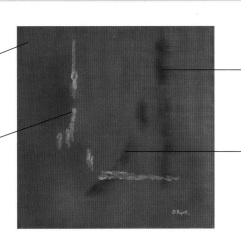

Second total cover with vermilion. Lines appear as a result of the brush strokes.

Add accents in chrome yellow and vermilion, applied very thickly.

Apply crimson and dark madder, and overpaint horizontally and vertically.

Various color solids are formed.

Step by step
Accents in blue

Plenty of paint and strong lines are also the basis for the third painting in the "fun with colors" series. The essential difference from the two previous works is that the first application is both complete and final.

Tangible forms now have a part to play—light and dark waves in the first coat and more significantly through the addition of dark blue accents in hard shapes that contrast with the waves.

Materials

Stretched canvas 20 x 16 inches (50 x 40 cm); household sponge; palette knife; jar of water; cotton cloth or paper towels; palette; colors: Prussian blue, chromium oxide green fiery, titanium white, and ultramarine; additive: glossy, heavy gel masking tape

Prussian blue

Chromium oxide green fiery

Titanium white

Ultramarine

1 On your palette, mix Prussian blue, chromium oxide green fiery, and a lot of white to make turquoise. Apply the paint to the canvas with a household sponge, wiping with diagonal wavy movements. Leave enough space at the top right and bottom left to add a different shade.

2 Now add a little ultramarine to the mixture and fill the top and bottom of the canvas in the same way.

3 The first coat is finished. The contrasts between light and dark tones of blue in the wave-forms are very beautiful.

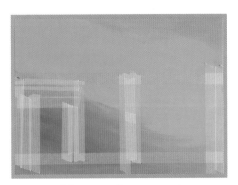

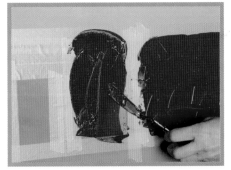

5 On your palette, mix a quantity of ultramarine paint with the glossy heavy gel additive in the proportion of approximately 50:50. Pick up the mixture with a palette knife and spread it over the open areas.

4 Measure the areas where you want to place the accents and stick enough masking tape around them to protect the other part of the painting.

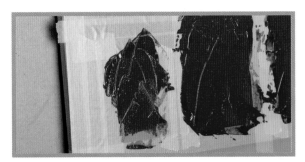

6 The heavy mixture means the paint you have applied will be quite solid and the spreading movements will create fine reliefs.

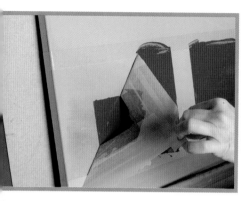

7 Now pull off the masking tape one piece at a time. Don't wait until the paint dries, as then you risk pulling it off with the tape.

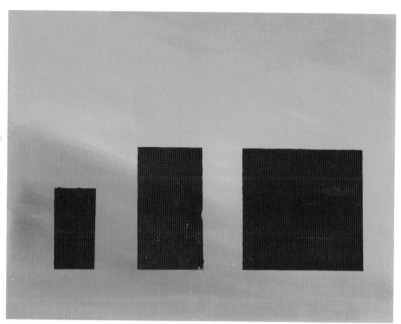

8 A wonderful symphony in blue has been created with simple means. The attraction lies in the contrast between the motion of the background and the strong, hard lines of the angular accents.

SUMMARY

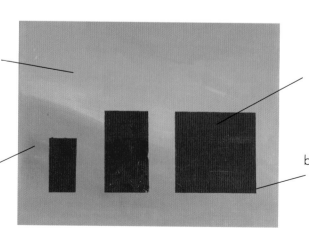

First stage of the background cover in turquoise waves in the middle of the painting.

Accents: heavy paint applied with a palette knife.

Second stage of the background cover with a darker blue at the top and bottom.

Straight lines are left behind when the tape is removed.

Still life

Ever since people in ancient times began painting pictures, the depiction of lifeless objects has been a favorite subject. In the Baroque period in the 17th and 18th centuries, still life was at its height. Constrained by strict rules of composition, it was carefully cultivated and developed to the peak of perfection. For newcomers to painting, still life is a very good way to approach the representation of objects.

DECIDE THE DEGREE OF DIFFICULTY FOR YOURSELF

The objects depicted artistically in a still life are inanimate and motionless. Some of them were once living (fruit, vegetables, animals); others were not (bottles, bowls, chairs etc.). Still life is very suitable for beginners, because the painter can determine the degree of difficulty for himself. The best way to begin is with an object that can be lit more or less from all sides, turn it this way and that, move it hither and thither, until you find the best arrangement. Then sketch the object before actually painting it. Gradually, as your confidence grows, the time will come for arranging a number of things in interesting groups.

A still life of five bottles placed centrally. The degree of difficulty in this case is already a bit higher. Apart from the outsides of the bottles, in two cases their transparency is also depicted.

OBJECTS WITH MEANING

Still life paintings have survived from Greek and Roman times. These were probably mainly for decorative purposes. The baroque age (1600–1790) is considered to be the golden age of the still life, when Dutch and Flemish artists in particular left their mark on the genre. Their aim was to convey, through the objects they painted, a symbolic hidden message that would give the beholder food for thought. For example, broken pots, bowls, and glasses were a symbol of earthly vanity, while the fading lights of oil lamps or candles referred to the passing of time and the inevitable eternal darkness of death. Grapes stood for Jesus Christ; the egg was a symbol of the resurrection. So the messages associated with the objects in these paintings had a marked religious content, and there were many more of these symbolic objects than are mentioned here.

However, around 1760, the still life was relieved of this heavy burden of symbolic meaning. From then on it was art for art's sake, for the sake of esthetics. The objects were now only used to convey color and form, which took over the leading role again.

Candle, skull, musical instrument, and shells are typical of the objects that carried messages in baroque still lifes. This picture from the year 2006 is an exercise that looks back to the old masters.

ARRANGEMENT AND COMPOSITION

No matter what period they come from, the same consideration has always been of outstanding importance: adherence to the rules of composition. For example, among the Netherlandish painters of around 1600, the components of a still life always had to be a vertical axis, a horizontal axis, and a spatial axis that reaches out into the room.

There are many options in composition. Incidentally, the word compose comes from the Latin "componere," meaning to put together. In painting, it's a matter of putting the elements together in a way that creates harmony, so that the positioning of an element or the arrangement of several is attractive. It's all about tension and balance.

An apple placed on two cloths, lying on a table. The main motif is to be found in the golden section, which gives the picture a particular tension.

COMPOSITION OPTIONS

First of all: compositional rules apply not only to still life but to every painting. However, it is true to say that composition plays a special part in still life.

At this point we want to present the most important kinds of composition.

- Central composition: the main motif is placed in the center of the picture.
- Triangular composition: the main motif or the elements form a triangle.
- Golden section: the golden section is created where a

horizontal and a vertical axis cross and are extended to around two thirds of the surface.

These three are the main options, but by no means the only ones. Objects standing next to one another (serial composition) can look just as attractive as a well-judged distribution composition.

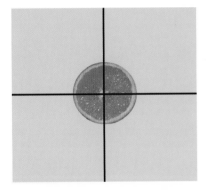

Central composition. *The main motif is in the center of the picture. It radiates peace, but can also appear boring.*

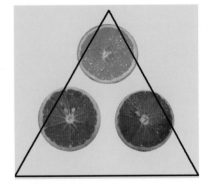

Triangular composition. *The main motif or the elements form a triangle. This type of composition was widespread in sacred art.*

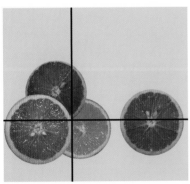

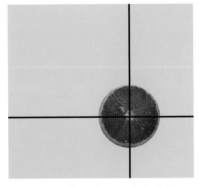

Golden section. *Theoretically it is found in four places in a picture, at the intersection of straight lines dividing the picture into unequal rectangles in a* proportion of approximately 8:13. The main motif or the majority of the elements are placed on or close to one of the four intersection points.

A painting that follows none of the rules of composition *looks arbitrary, and is often irritating as well.*

Special
Preliminary sketch

If you want to achieve good results in representational painting, a preliminary sketch on the support is very important. It will allow you to fix the outlines and contours of the still life, landscape, figure etc. that you will be painting later. When you work on it with paint, these are important clues for keeping the proportions and the details of the content correct. Preliminary sketches have the additional advantage that you can go on correcting them until you are satisfied all the details are right.

You can either transfer the content from an original using the grid method as described on pages 28–29, or draw freehand on the support.

Pencil is perfect *for working out the details of a figure.*

A graphite stick is good for transferring *the content of a picture using a grid, and also for freehand drawing.*

Fine lines, but almost impossible to erase: *a preliminary drawing in red chalk. The lines will mix with the first application of acrylic paint.*

FROM PENCIL TO PAINTBRUSH

There are various drawing implements that can be used to make a preliminary sketch. We would like to introduce you to five of them here.

- Pencil: the most frequently used drawing implement for sketches and, of course, preliminary drawings. It is important that the pencil should be soft, for instance "b" or "2b". Advantages: it can always be rubbed out to make corrections, and the outlines are fine.
- Graphite stick: next to pencil, the most important drawing implement for grid transfers. It is softer than pencil and the lines are a bit thicker. Both can, of course, also be used for freehand drawing.
- Red chalk: similar to a graphite stick in covering strength. A red chalk drawing looks more delicate, but is almost impossible to rub out. The lines will mix visibly with thin applications of acrylic paint. This can produce attractive effects and has the advantage that the contours fade and the design becomes freer.
- Natural charcoal: wood that has been turned into charcoal is very soft and very good for freehand drawing. You can make corrections by wiping it off and drawing over it again. In a preliminary sketch, you can already determine light and shade. Charcoal must be fixed with a special charcoal and pastel fixative from a spray can, preferably in several thin coats, until no more will rub off.
- Paintbrush: more experienced artists can also make preliminary sketches with a brush. The outlines are painted delicately with acrylic paint thinned with a lot of water. Use a single color for this, or two at most.

In a preliminary sketch using a brush, *it's important to outline the contours with verve and capture the essentials. The lower picture shows the first color added in green.*

Drawn freehand with charcoal, *the light and shade values (chiaroscuro) are already determined.*

Step by step
Plate of grapes

A plate filled with black grapes gives you an easy start in this genre. The objects are arranged symmetrically, the light falls from the top right and determines the values of light and shade. The arrangement is in the category of central compositions. In this picture, only four colors are used, from which all the necessary shades are mixed. This makes the plate of grapes a very good practice exercise for getting the right colors.

Materials
Stretched canvas 12 x 12 inches (30 x 30 cm); pencil; graphite stick; fixative; flat brush no. 8; jar of water; cotton cloth or paper towels; palette; colors: vermilion, ultramarine, cadmium yellow light, and titanium white

Vermilion

Ultramarine

Cadmium yellow light

Titanium white

Advice
Always begin your picture with the main subject, for the preliminary drawing, when you start painting, and even more when it comes to the finishing touches. The most important always comes first—it makes the picture more alive.

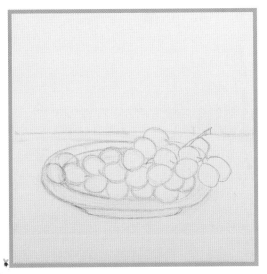

1 Make a preliminary drawing of the plate and the grapes in fine pencil and then thicken the lines with the graphite stick. Spray the graphite layer with fixative. Take care that some of the grapes overlap one another, not all lying separately.

2 Mix the vermilion and ultramarine to a violet shade. Thin the paint with a lot of water and paint the grapes. Clean the brush with water and gently wipe it dry. Now use the brush to take off some of the wet paint from the top halves of the grapes. The lighter patches will give an impression of three-dimensionality. For the stalks, mix cadmium yellow light with ultramarine, which gives a fresh green. For the plate, mix titanium white with a little cadmium yellow light, a very small amount of vermilion, and a trace of ultramarine. This gives a very pale shade of beige to gray.

Tip

So far, we have applied the paint as a glaze (transparent). It is worth considering whether to give the painting a further glazing coat to finish with. This is entirely a matter of the artist's taste. We have decided to paint it opaque.

3 Block in the table in a pale orange, mixed from cadmium yellow light, a little vermilion, and titanium white. Give the shadow under the plate a violet tint. That way you create a little contrast between the colors, which produces a three-dimensional effect. Block in the background with the pale violet shade and the delicate yellowy orange as well.

4 Mix ultramarine with a very little vermilion to give a violet blue, but this time without adding any water, and paint the bottom halves of the grapes.

5 Add a little more vermilion to the violet blue to make a reddish violet. Break up the top edge of the violet blue a little with this color and mix the two.

6 Now mix titanium white into the violet and paint the upper side of the grapes. Blur the transition between the dark and light violet tones.

7 To add slight contrasts, paint the underside of one or two grapes with a mixture of cadmium yellow light, a little ultramarine, and titanium white. Use this light, fresh green for the stalks as well.

8 Paint the upper edge of the plate with a light beige, mixed from titanium white, a very little cadmium yellow light, and a trace of vermilion. Paint the light parts of the edge of the plate and leave out the areas shaded by the grapes.

9 The color of the shadow falling on the plate is mixed as follows: into the beige you used for the edge of the plate, mix a little more vermilion and cadmium yellow light, and to make it darker a little ultramarine. This gives a slightly faded beige-gray.

10 Now add carefully placed points of light and shade. With a little titanium white and ultramarine you can create more spatial depth.

11 From cadmium yellow light, vermilion, and a little titanium white mix the color for the table, a bright orange, which you apply flat. You make the color for the shadow of the plate with the same orange, with less titanium white, and a little ultramarine. The brush strokes should be horizontal.

12 The background is made up of two mixtures of color: the sides of a very pale violet and the middle above the curve of the grapes of a very pale cadmium yellow light. The brush strokes should be vertical.

SUMMARY

Grapes: create the three-dimensional effect with layers of violet, green, white, and a little light blue.

Shadows of the grapes with a slightly faded beige-gray.

Background of two color mixtures and vertical brush strokes.

When painting the table, the brush strokes are horizontal.

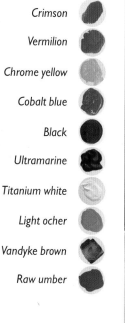

Step by step
Apple

Our second still life picture is a simple subject. It shows an apple positioned on two cloths on a table. It uses the golden section to introduce tension into the picture. A light source illuminates the fruit from above left. The subject makes it possible to concentrate on the details of the apple. The cloths and the table are painted flat.

Crimson

Vermilion

Chrome yellow

Cobalt blue

Black

Ultramarine

Titanium white

Light ocher

Vandyke brown

Raw umber

Materials

Stretched canvas 12 x 12 inches (30 x 30 cm); graphite stick; fixative; flat brush no. 10; round brush size 6; jar of water; cotton cloth or paper towels; palette; colors: crimson, vermilion, chrome yellow, cobalt blue, black, ultramarine, titanium white, light ocher, Vandyke brown, and raw umber.

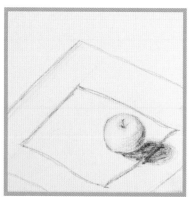

1 When making the preliminary drawing, pay attention to the circular shape of the apple and the position of the stalk in the hollow. Also draw in both the shadow of the stalk and the apple. This already produces a three-dimensional effect. Complete the preliminary drawing with the outlines of the cloths.

2 Mix a red shade from crimson and vermilion. Paint the body of the apple following the natural rounded shape of the fruit with the flat brush. Every now and then, use the two shades of red separately.

3 Add a green tone, by mixing chrome yellow, a little cobalt blue, and a trace of vermilion, and paint in volume the parts that are still white. Don't use just one mixture, but sometimes add a little more chrome yellow and sometimes a little more cobalt blue.

4 The shadow cast by the apple is an element of the painting in its own right. For the shadow on the white cloth, mix titanium white with black, a little ultramarine, and a trace of crimson. For the ocher-colored cloth, use a mixture of light ocher and Vandyke brown, plus some cobalt blue and a little ultramarine. Next, block in the two different shadow areas with the appropriate colors.

Give the side of the apple away from the light some of the shadow color for the white tablecloth to represent the mutual reflections of the apple and the cloth.

Advice

Shadows are special pictorial elements in painting. To get the right color for the shadows, we have the following rule: mix a darker shade of the local color with its complementary color and a little ultramarine.

An example: the local color of a tomato is vermilion. For the shadow, you take a darker red, crimson for example, mix it with the complementary color of the local color, which is a turquoise green, and add a trace of ultramarine.

5 Now paint the smaller cloth in titanium white and a little light ocher, and the larger one in light ocher with a little titanium white, applying the paint flat. Paint over the graphite of the preliminary drawing to create the edges of the shadows.

6 Block in the table in the background with Vandyke brown and raw umber.

7 Now go over the surfaces of the cloths with the same colors in a thicker consistency.

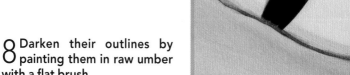

8 Darken their outlines by painting them in raw umber with a flat brush.

9 Finish off the apple and darken the shadows in the hollow, and the shadow cast by the stalk.

10 Paint over the background again with the mixture of Vandyke brown and raw umber.

11 Using the round brush and titanium white, add highlights to the stalk and the body of the apple.

12 Although this still life only consists of a single main element, the work needed to bring out small details offers interesting challenges.

SUMMARY

Paint the apple following its contours in shades of red and green.

Add shadows.

Paint the cloths with two coats of white and ocher.

Finally, add highlights in white.

Light and shade

Our still life creates the interplay of light and shade using a stepladder and two chairs. With this kind of subject, you can capture everyday life in an artistic way—the content of a still life doesn't always have to consist of classic objects. The shadows on the floor and wall offer a new challenge after the exercise with the apple. Of course the background is not left completely white but is given structure by the careful painting of the shadows.

Materials

Stretched canvas 24 x 32 inches (60 x 80 cm); graphite stick; flat brush no. 10; round brush size 6; jar of water; cotton cloth or paper towels; palette; colors: Vandyke brown, titanium white, crimson, black, and ultramarine

 Vandyke brown

Titanium white

 Crimson

 Black

Ultramarine

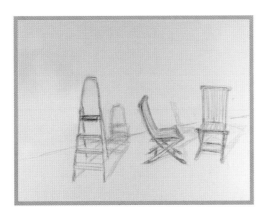

1 The preliminary sketch using a graphite stick already shows all the objects. No fixative is used. A single source of light means that the shadows fall at slightly different angles.

59

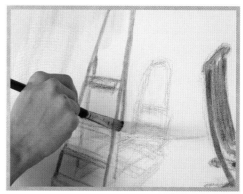

2 Paint the outlines of the chairs in Vandyke brown. Where the chair legs cross, take care to leave gaps in the parts that go behind and only paint those in front in full.

3 To block in the stepladder, paint over the graphite with a wet brush and titanium white.

4 Block in the shadows of the chairs and the stepladder by painting over the preliminary sketch with a wet brush.

5 The first application of color for the chairs, stepladder, and shadows is complete. The graphite of the preliminary drawing is incorporated in the same way for the floor and wall.

6 Paint the floor and wall with titanium white rather more completely, working the graphite in further.

7 Block in the plastic parts of the stepladder with a glazing of crimson.

8 Paint the chairs in more detail, using mixtures of Vandyke brown and black.

9 The painting after the floor, wall, and chairs have been painted in detail and the stepladder blocked in.

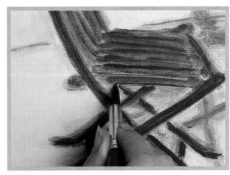

10 Put in the details of the stepladder in impasto, using crimson for the plastic parts and titanium white on the light areas, and add highlights. Then put in the detail of the darkest bits with a mixture of Vandyke brown and black.

11 Now it's the turn of the darkest bits of the chairs, also with a mixture of Vandyke brown and black.

12 To finish off the shadows, mix black, titanium white, and a trace of ultramarine.

13 Lastly, finish off the floor and walls between the shadows and the objects with titanium white, with a little black mixed in.

14 Paint the large areas of floor and wall with the same mixture. The brush strokes should be vertical for the wall and horizontal for the floor.

SUMMARY

The depiction of the shadows creates an impression of space.

Detailing the lightest and darkest parts.

Red parts as spots of color.

Wall and floor contrasted by brush strokes in opposite directions.

Outlines of the chairs in Vandyke brown.

Five bottles

Four of the five bottles in our next still life were actually transparent in the original arrangement. In order not to set the degree of difficulty too high, only two are depicted as transparent. Painting bottles involves one or two particular skills. The most important is to get their curves onto the support in the correct perspective (page 64).

To do this, you block in cylindrical objects with opening or closing circles and ellipses, depending on the perspective.

 Light ocher

 Ultramarine

Cadmium yellow light

 Vermilion

 Chromium oxide green fiery

 Titanium white

Materials

Stretched canvas 20 x 20 inches (50 x 50 cm); natural charcoal; fixative; flat brush no. 12; jar of water; cotton cloth or paper towels; palette; colors: light ocher, ultramarine, cadmium yellow light, vermilion, chromium oxide green fiery, and titanium white

5 Still life

1 Before you start the preliminary drawing, arrange the bottles and make a sketch in order to establish the proportions and perspective. For each bottle, first draw a cylinder and its central axis. Draw the ellipses representing the bottom, body, and neck of the bottle around this midpoint.

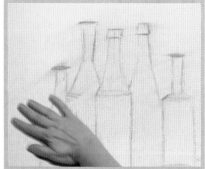

2 Transfer the sketch to the support in charcoal. Rub out the first versions with the flat of your hand and keep drawing the outlines until you are satisfied with the result.

3 Block in the shadows as part of the charcoal sketch. You can put in shadows by rubbing with your fingers. Spray the sketch with fixative several times, until no more charcoal rubs off.

4 With a household sponge, apply light ocher thinned with a lot of water. This kind of application is called imprimatura.

5 Begin with the bottle at the front. Mix a bluish-gray shade from cadmium yellow light, vermilion, ultramarine, and titanium white, and paint the first parts of the bottle following its structure.

6 Add a little more ultramarine to the mixture and paint the areas where the blue of the other bottles shines through. Use titanium white to put in the lightest accents on the bottles.

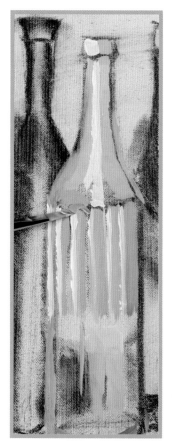

Advice

A wash (or imprimatura) completely covers the support and gives the picture a background color. Depending on your intentions, it may harmonize with the major colors, but it can also be in contrast to them.

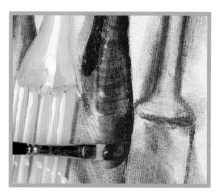

7 Paint the second bottle that is just to the right of the first in pure ultramarine, following its contours. For the left-hand half, darken the blue by adding black.

Tip
To get the exact shade for the two outer bottles, add a little chromium oxide green fiery to the mixture of titanium white and ultramarine.

8 Finally, put in highlights with titanium white.

9 The blue of the second bottle from the left shines through the bottle on the far left. When you paint this bottle, use some of its color, a mixture of ultramarine and titanium white, in the first bottle as well.

10 When you have finished all the bottles, paint the table with a mixture of titanium white, light ocher, and a little vermilion. You can capture the reflection of the bottles in the surface of the table by using vertical brush strokes and the colors of each of the bottles.

11 For the background, use light ocher mixed with titanium white. The shadows of the bottles on the wall are a special part of the picture. Mix the appropriate color from light ocher, with less titanium white than before, and add a little blue—the complementary color of ocher—and a hint of ultramarine as usual.

12 A very expressive still life has been created with five bottles. The color contrast between ocher and blue gives a pleasant, fresh effect that is not at all cold, despite the large amount of blue.

SUMMARY

Paint the bottles following their contours or structure.

Bring out the transparency of a bottle.

Vertical brush strokes for the reflections; horizontal brush strokes for the tabletop.

Reflections and shadows enhance the three-dimensional effect.

Basket of vegetables

A still life with objects that are classic for this genre is the last work in our series. However, the various vegetables aren't conveying any kind of message, they're just arranged and painted for their own sakes. Vari-ous shapes and different colors make the picture very complex and offer quite a challenge. All the same, their soft curves allow plenty of freedom in the way they are represented.

Materials

Stretched canvas 20 x 28 inches (50 x 70 cm); graphite stick; fixative; flat brush no. 12; round brush size 6; jar of water; cotton cloth or paper towels; palette; colors: light ocher, Prussian blue, chromium oxide green fiery, vermilion, dark madder, titanium white, and ultramarine

Light ocher

Prussian blue

Chromium oxide green fiery

Vermilion

Dark madder

Ultramarine

Titanium white

1 The preliminary drawing shows the true proportions and distribution of the vegetables. Draw with a graphite stick, then spray with fixative until no more rubs off.

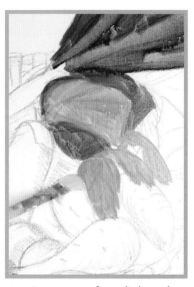

2 mix a green from light ocher, Prussian blue, chromium oxide green fiery, and a little vermilion. Use this to block in the darkest areas, e.g. the savoy and the tops of the leeks. Then add titanium white to the mixture to produce a lighter green.

3 The green vegetables have been blocked in. The brush strokes already follow the form and contours at this stage. Leave spaces on the leaves to add the veins later (step 11).

4 With a mixture of vermilion and dark madder, block in the onions. For the sweet potatoes, add a little titanium white. Paint these vegetables with brush strokes that follow the contours.

Tip

For very dark areas of a picture, mix what is known as a classic black from Prussian blue, dark madder, and chromium oxide green fiery.

5 From vermilion, Prussian blue, and a very little light ocher, mix a grayish violet and block in the eggplant. Add highlights in titanium white. For the mushrooms, use a light brown shade, mixed from light ocher, Prussian blue, vermilion, and a lot of titanium white.

6 To paint the folds of the cloth, mix light ocher and titanium white, and break it up with a little dark madder. Darken the color in stages by adding a trace of Prussian blue each time.

7 Block in the basket with light ocher, Prussian blue, and vermilion. Follow the structure of its surface with your brush strokes.

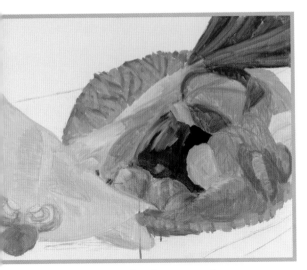

8 The elements in the foreground are now blocked in. The lighter areas of the basket were produced by adding titanium white to the original mixture (step 7).

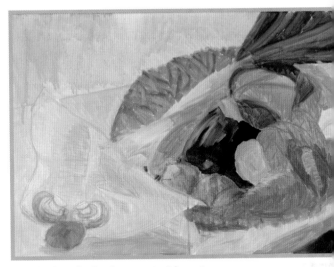

9 Block in the background with a mixture of titanium white, a little dark madder, and a little Prussian blue. The table was given a first coat of titanium white with a little Prussian blue to add contrast to the picture.

10 Now finish off the vegetables, with the same colors as when blocking in, but with a buttery consistency. Begin with the darkest areas, for instance on the leeks, and gradually lighten the tone by adding more titanium white.

11 Finish the leaves with brush strokes following the contours. You previously left spaces for the veins of the leaves.

Tip
Vary the shades of green by changing the proportions of the individual colors light ocher, titanium white, vermilion, and Prussian blue.

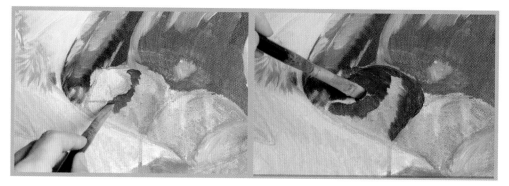

12 Next, finish the onions with vermilion, following their structure. Then add dark madder. For the lighter areas in the middle, mix the madder with some titanium white. The colors are still wet. Using a flat brush with no paint, draw fine lines from dark to light and vice versa. This will produce the typical structures of a red onion.

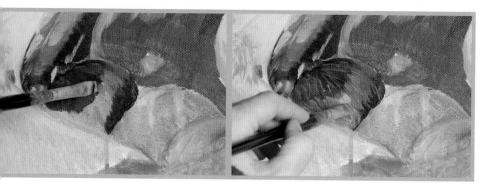

13 Work with the color mixture for the eggplant (step 5) in a buttery consistency, following the contours. For the lighter areas you again add titanium white. The lightest areas consist of pure titanium white.

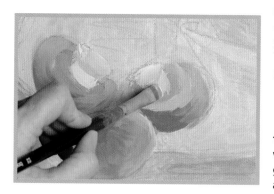

14 Finish the mushrooms in the same mixture as for blocking in (step 5). Begin with the darkest areas and gradually lighten the tone by adding more titanium white. Create the structure of the mushrooms by drawing the flat brush without paint from light to dark and vice versa.

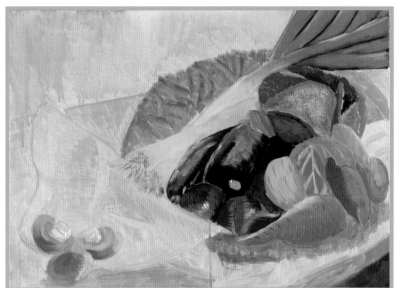

15 The vegetables are finished.

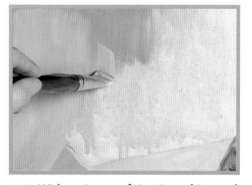

16 To finish the cloth, use the
color mixture as in step 6, in
a buttery consistency. The direction of your brush strokes depends
on how the cloth is lying.

17 Now finish the basket with the color
mixture from step 7, following the
structure. Gradually lighten the tone by
adding more titanium white.

18 With a mixture of titanium white, and
a little dark madder and ultramarine,
finish off the background, using vertical
brush strokes. The light violet echoes the
violet of the eggplant.

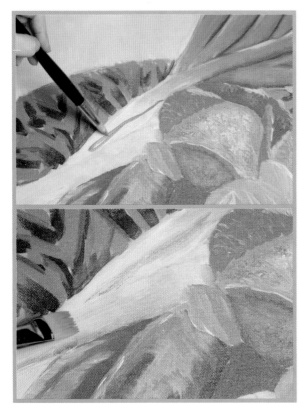

19 After the picture has been completely finished in thick paint, we pick out the important points in dark and light. For the dark green of the leeks, use the color mixture from step 2, thinned with water, and the round brush. Lastly, smear the paint with a dry flat brush.

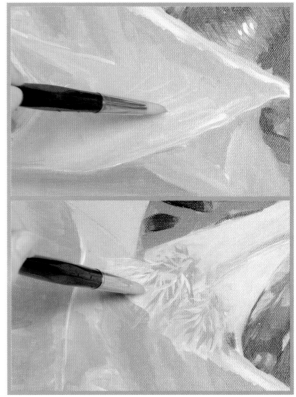

20 Put in the highlights with titanium white, using the round brush. This gives you an additional opportunity to emphasize the finer structures.

21 The color coat on the table has been completely painted over, with the color for the basket (step 7), plus titanium white and the addition of light ocher as necessary. The brush strokes correspond to the diagonal view of the table. Work from light to dark, and finish by emphasizing the darkest and lightest areas once more to give the whole thing more depth.

SUMMARY

Paint the vegetables with smooth surfaces following their contours.

Paint the darkest areas with classic black.

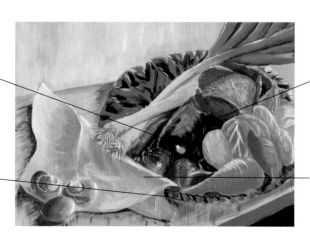

Paint the basket and vegetables with rough surfaces following their structure.

Light and shade enhance the three-dimensional effect.

Plants

6

Plants are living things—so the most important difference from the still life genre is immediately obvious. The enjoyment of nature, trees, bushes, grasses, flowers, and so on is a great source of motivation for a painter to turn to plants. In fact, you will not find that greens and browns predominate, because the multiplicity of flowers offers a feast of color, as do the changing seasons. The countless different shapes and structures will provide you with an extra challenge.

IN A GREEN SHADE

Green is, of course, a color, but how many shades of green are there? The answer is simple: it's actually impossible to count them. Yet the various greens are the most important colors when it comes to plants. This is because the chlorophyll used by plants for photosynthesis in order to stay alive is green. However, the local color plays a subordinate role in perception. The many shades are produced mainly by the effects of light and shade, brightness and darkness. Leaves that are the same shade of green may take on a vast number of apparent colors, from almost black to something approaching white. It's true that plants are green—but how green?

Green is also considered to be the most difficult color in painting. We have paid tribute to that by devoting a special page to green (page 92).

Trees are also green—that's obvious. But that's not the whole story. They delight us with their many different shapes, the structure of their bark, their grandeur, and their vital energy. So it is not surprising that they are among the favorite subjects for painters when it comes to the theme of "plants."

The leaf of a plant is green —but how green? Tonal values ranging from almost white to nearly black are possible.

A splendid weeping willow bows down into the water.

VARIETY OF FORM

Lovers of form get their money's worth from plants. The curving leaves of a tulip are simple and elegant, while its slender stalk rises straight up and merges into a beautiful calyx. This flower, which came to Europe via Persia, was considered a luxury in the Middle Ages and was valued more highly than gold or precious stones. If you examine one closely, you can understand why.

Plants en masse have quite a different effect. At first glance, you can only get an overall impression of a meadow full of wild flowers and grasses. The details only become apparent when you take a second look, and you see "individuals," each one, without exception, raising its head proudly toward the sun.

Simple, clear, and elegant: *the tulip's beauty is captivating.*

Grasses and flowers *in a summer meadow.*

EVERYTHING IS COLORFUL!

Being eye-catching is a way of getting ahead in life, and it works for flowers. They make use of a whole palette of striking colors in shades of red, yellow, and blue in order to catch the attention of the insects that will guarantee their propagation. Their magnificent and exciting shapes also make them a feast for the eye—particularly for painters. A beautiful, brightly colored flower makes an ideal subject. Small wonder, then, that flowers are always top of the pops.

The sunflower *was once worshiped by the Incas as an image of their god.*

Special
First things first!

In representational painting, the usual order of events is: preliminary drawing, first application of paint watery, second application impasto, then emphasizing the darkest, and finally the lightest areas. But if you want to paint vivid pictures, you should follow one more rule, right from the start of the preliminary drawing. This rule says: "Begin with the most important thing, with what is in the foreground, what matters to you!" This is not necessarily the same for every painter.

A picture conveys the artist's idea, and his intention will only come to life if he has worked on the main element right from the start. That way the objects and other elements in the picture will have the intended effect and give the painting clarity and power.

FROM FOREGROUND TO BACKGROUND

Concentrating on the foreground, the important elements of the picture, and sticking to the correct order for blocking in and adding detail will help you to avoid typical mistakes, such as blocking in the entire sky and only then adding trees that reach up into the sky. The result is that the colors of the trees mix with those of the sky, not just in the literal sense, but also because the colors overlie one another and thus lose some of their strength and brilliance. Structures from a different set of brush strokes show through. In short, what should stand out appears faded and dull. The quality of the picture is reduced.

To show you the correct procedure, we have chosen an example; a few ivy leaves against a wall. We want the ivy to dominate the foreground and the wall to be merely the background, so this is how we proceed.

1 After the preliminary drawing—which began with the ivy—start by blocking in the green of the ivy leaves.

2 The foreground is blocked in with the first color.

3 Now, it's the turn of all the parts of the background immediately adjacent to the foreground, including any shadows.

4 Now follows the second application, with the brush strokes following the leaf structures.

5 Finish the leaves before applying the second coat to the background.

6 Begin the second application to the background, immediately next to and between the leaves.

7 Emphasizing the darkest areas and putting in highlights increases the brilliance of the foreground and makes the leaves stand out even more from the background.

An elegant tulip

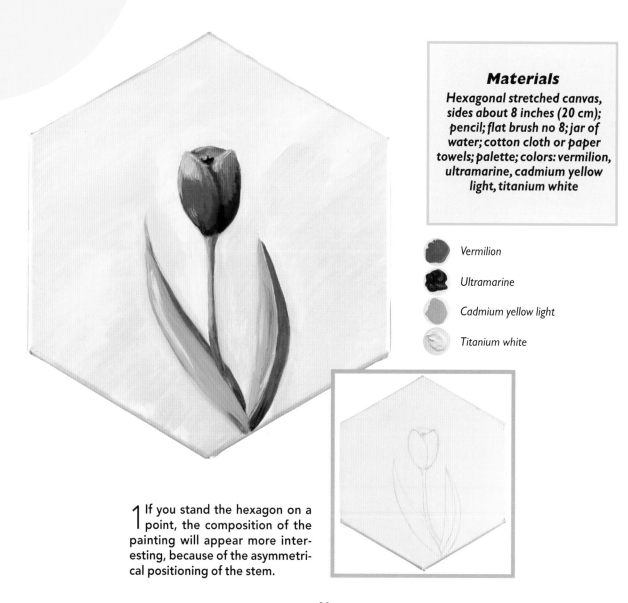

Painting a tulip is a great way to start on the subject of "plants." Firstly, its simple beauty offers great esthetic pleasure, and secondly, its forms are easy to reproduce. Incidentally, did you know that there was once a period of "tulipomania?" In Holland in the 1730s, three tulip bulbs were once worth as much as an entire house. The dream of riches collapsed, but the beauty of the tulip remains.

Materials

Hexagonal stretched canvas, sides about 8 inches (20 cm); pencil; flat brush no 8; jar of water; cotton cloth or paper towels; palette; colors: vermilion, ultramarine, cadmium yellow light, titanium white

Vermilion

Ultramarine

Cadmium yellow light

Titanium white

1 If you stand the hexagon on a point, the composition of the painting will appear more interesting, because of the asymmetrical positioning of the stem.

2 With a mixture of vermilion, ultramarine, and a little titanium white, block in the lower edges of the petals in violet. Paint the main areas of the flower in vermilion, and the tips of the petals in cadmium yellow light.

3 Block in the stem and leaves with a mixture of cadmium yellow light, ultramarine, and titanium white for light areas. For darker parts, mix a little vermilion into the green.

4 At the center of the flower, paint the pistil in a dark violet, mixed from vermilion and ultramarine. Block in the background with plenty of titanium white and a little vermilion and ultramarine, using diagonal brush strokes.

5 Second application with thicker paint. Begin with the lower edges of the petals, using the same violet as for blocking in. After that, it's the turn of the main parts of the petals in vermilion, while the tips are finished off with cadmium yellow light.

Tip

Apply the second layer of paint wet-into-wet, i.e. immediately after the first. After applying the yellow, clean the brush in water and dry it gently. Then drag it over all three colors, following the shape of the flower, so the colors mingle a little, creating a fluid transition from one to the other.

6 Paint the petal at the back in more detail and finish the darkest parts of the calyx.

7 Finish the light areas of the leaves with the same color mixture as for step 3 but with thick paint. Do the same for the darkest parts, but using less titanium white.

8 Finish the background wet-into-wet with a lot of titanium white and a little ultramarine, cadmium yellow light, and vermilion. Stick to the same diagonal brush strokes you used for blocking in. With titanium white, put in the highlights on the flower and the leaves.

SUMMARY

Paint the calyx wet-into-wet and smear.

Background with diagonal brush strokes.

Contrast the color of the leaves and the stem.

Add highlights in titanium white.

Sunflower

Brought back from America by Spanish seafarers, the sunflower has long since become an important agricultural and decorative plant. The challenge—and the pleasure—of painting it consist in capturing the individual nature of a sunflower and transferring it to the canvas. With its strong colors, large flower head, and generously filled seed head, it symbolizes life and fertility. It radiates friendliness and seems somehow human.

Materials

Stretched canvas 24 x 32 inches (60 x 80 cm); graphite stick; fixative; flat brushes nos. 18 and 32; jar of water; cotton cloth or paper towels; palette; colors: cadmium yellow light, vermilion, ultramarine, chromium oxide green fiery, titanium white

Cadmium yellow light

Vermilion

Ultramarine

Chromium oxide green fiery

Titanium white

1 Draw the preliminary sketch with a graphite stick and then spray with fixative until no more rubs off.

2 First application using cadmium yellow light. Block in the lightest parts of the petals.

3 Add a very little vermilion to the cadmium yellow light to give a light orange. Use this to block in the darker parts of the petals and the edge of the seed head.

Tip
Keep adding vermilion to create a bright orange. For the leaves in the shadow, mix a little ultramarine into the orange.

4 Block in the seed head in a green mixed from cadmium yellow light and ultramarine. For darker areas, add a little chromium oxide green fiery.

5 Block in the dark green of the stem with the same mixture as for the seed head, and the background in titanium white with the addition of a very little ultramarine.

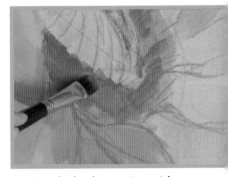

6 Finish the petals with a second coat, first with cadmium yellow light, then, as described in step 3, with the addition of more and more vermilion.

7 Mix a little ultramarine with the dark orange and finish the edge of the seed head with the brush strokes, following the structure.

9 Paint the light part of the seed head with a mixture of cadmium yellow light and ultramarine.

8 With the same mixture as in step 7, paint the petals that are in shadow and the dark area of the seed head.

10 The second, impasto, coat is complete. You can repeat it as often as you think necessary, so the paint covers better and the painting acquires greater depth and intensity of color.

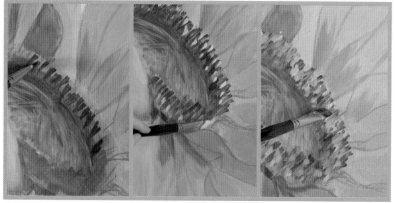

11 Now finish off the other elements of the seed head one by one, working from dark to light. Begin with the mixture from step 7, but with a higher proportion of ultramarine. Then it's the turn of titanium white, and finally a few dabs of cadmium yellow light.

12 With the mixture from step 11, emphasize the darkest areas.

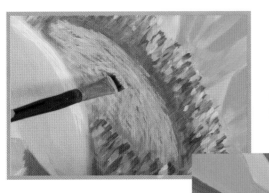

13 Add highlights in titanium white, broken with a trace of cadmium yellow light.

14 Finish the background using thick titanium white and a little ultramarine. This includes all the major light patches near the stem.

SUMMARY

For petals in shadow, add a little ultramarine to the orange.

Very pale blue of the background contrasting with the petals.

Seed head painted following the structure.

Petals in cadmium yellow light, with gradually increasing amounts of vermilion.

Colorful flower meadow

The wide variety of different species is an important characteristic of a lush flower meadow. Countless different grasses grow side by side, competing for sunlight. Poppies, marguerites, dandelions, daisies, buttercups, and many other flowers offer spots of color from all parts of the spectrum. Depending on the viewpoint and the weather, a dramatic sky can add particular accents. The painter's task is to create an interesting composition from the many details.

Materials

Stretched canvas 12 x 12 inches (30 x 30 cm); pencil; fixative; household sponge; flat brushes nos. 10 and 18; round brushes sizes 4 and 8; jar of water; cotton cloth or paper towels; palette; colors: chrome yellow, vermilion, Prussian blue, titanium white, crimson, ultramarine, cadmium yellow light, black

Chrome yellow

Vermilion

Prussian blue

Titanium white

Crimson

Ultramarine

Cadmium yellow light

Black

1 In the preliminary drawing, pencil in the outlines of the most important plants. Spray with fixative until no more rubs off.

2 With a household sponge, apply a thin, watery mixture of chrome yellow and vermilion. This wash gives the picture a warm background color.

3 Block in the grasses and flower stems with various mixtures of chrome yellow, vermilion, and Prussian blue, lightened with titanium white as required.

 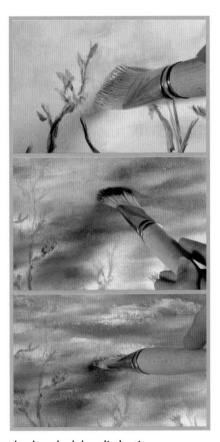

4 With the background wash and the first layer of color on the grasses and flowers, this phase is completed.

5 Paint the sky in three phases. Begin with a mixture of titanium white and a little Prussian blue. Then add a little more Prussian blue and a little crimson to the mixture to produce a blue with a hint of violet. Finally, with a very

dry brush dab a little titanium white onto the sky. The background wash should be allowed to shine through in places.

6 Now you have finished blocking in the sky as well as the plants.

7 Finish the grasses using the same colors as for step 3. You can also add ultramarine and cadmium yellow light to the mixture.

Advice

You can create a particularly interesting effect by picking up pure individual colors on your brush and applying them with sweeping strokes. The colors will mix to some extent.

Ultramarine, vermilion, and cadmium yellow light *picked up on the brush and applied without mixing.*

8 In this step, finish off the flowers with chrome yellow and vermilion. For this—without taking it too far—you can also use the technique described on the left, i.e. using the two colors unmixed on the brush.

9 Darken the greens of steps 3 and 7 with black to emphasize the darkest parts of the flowers and grasses.

10 Add the final accents by painting the light parts of the flowers and grasses with an opaque mixture of chrome yellow and a little vermilion, and in selected places with pure chrome yellow or vermilion.

11 Add a few more flowers and grasses until you get the desired three-dimensional effect. Then finish the sky with titanium white, Prussian blue, a little vermilion, and a little chrome yellow.

SUMMARY

Dramatic sky.

Paint the contours of the plants in detail.

Make the flowers shine out.

Warm background color as a wash.

Special
Shades of green

When it's a question of mixing colors for painting, greens are among the more difficult. If you experiment with using a green straight from the tube or the jar to paint a whole area of a tree, a bush, or a meadow, you will soon discover that the green looks unnatural. So to create natural-looking shades of green, you should mix them from other colors.

BLUE AND YELLOW

Before you start mixing greens, set out all the blue and yellow paints you have. After all, according to color theory, blue and yellow make green.

The yellows used in this book are primary yellow, cadmium yellow light, chrome yellow, and light ocher. The blues are ultramarine, cobalt blue, and Prussian blue.

Now you can—and should—lay out a color grid as described on pages 22 and 23 with greens mixed from the different blues and yellows.

If you now feel prompted to ask why you should buy any green paints at all, the answer is simple: to mix them with other colors to produce (more) natural shades of green. So you should add mixtures of chromium oxide green fiery and chromium oxide green opaque to the blues and yellows and their mixtures on your color grid.

A view of the Gardens of Eyrignac in the South of France—photo and painting.

AND RED AS WELL!

To make greens produced by mixing look even more natural, you often need to "break" them by adding a red. In this way you can get more warmth into the green and also produce shades that tend toward brown.

Greens are often broken using vermilion, which hardly seems likely when you consider what a bright red it is. However, other shades of red are also used, ranging from crimson and madder to reddish browns such as burnt sienna.

And of course you can darken or lighten any shade with black or white (page 23).

To illustrate this topic, we have taken a photo of a park as a model and turned it into a painting. Here are a few examples of how we went about mixing the colors.

1 Darken chromium oxide green opaque with black for the dark parts of the hedges. For the light areas, mix chromium oxide green opaque and light ocher.

2 For the fresh green of the lawns, mix primary yellow and cobalt blue.

3 For the dark parts of the trees on the left, mix Prussian blue and light ocher, and break the green with a touch of vermilion. For the lighter parts of the trees, add cobalt blue and primary yellow to the mixture.

4 The color for the trees in the background is mixed from Prussian blue, titanium white, and a little light ocher.

Weeping willow by the lake

For those of us who live in temperate regions, vegetation without trees is unimaginable. With their combination of roots, trunks, branches, twigs, leaves, and sometimes fruits, trees are among the most impressive plants we know. The weeping willow in our picture really exists in a park in Brussels. In a strange way it has bent down almost into the water, as though it wanted to drink from the little lake. It makes a fantastic subject for artists, which we have captured on canvas in 16 steps.

Materials

Stretched canvas 24 x 32 inches (60 x 80 cm); graphite stick; flat brush no. 18; round brush size 6; jar of water; cotton cloth or paper towels; palette; colors: chromium oxide green opaque, titanium white, cadmium yellow light, light ocher, vermilion, ultramarine, Prussian blue, chromium oxide green fiery, dark madder

Chromium oxide green opaque

Titanium white

Cadmium yellow light

Light ocher

Vermilion

Ultramarine

Prussian blue

Chromium oxide green fiery

Dark madder

1 Draw the outline of the tree in graphite stick, but don't spray with fixative. The reflections and shadows can already be seen, as well as indications of the background.

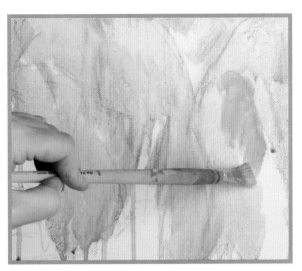

2 Block in the darkest parts of the crown of the tree with chromium oxide green opaque. For the lighter parts, gradually add more titanium white.

3 Add a little cadmium yellow light to the lightest green mixture and use it to block in the yellowish areas of the treetop and the grass.

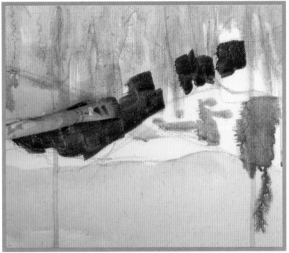

4 For the darkest areas of water underneath the tree, use a mixture of Prussian blue, light ocher, and a little vermilion.

5 For the tree trunk, use a mixture of Prussian blue, chromium oxide green fiery, and dark madder. Paint with brush strokes following the structure.

6 Emphasize the darkest parts of the crown by dabbing with a mixture of chromium oxide green opaque and vermilion. Block in the background in delicate shades of green mixed with a lot of water. The lightest, pale blue reflections in the water are created with a mixture of titanium white and a little Prussian blue.

7 After adding detail to the dark parts of the crown, use a mixture of chromium oxide green opaque with a little ultramarine and titanium white to finish the lighter parts. Dab on the paint with the brush following the structure of the crown. The spots should be closer together in the darker parts. Put a few dark spots in the light areas and vice versa. The lightest mixture consists of ultramarine, cadmium yellow light, a little chromium oxide green opaque, and titanium white. Using a dry brush and a very little titanium white, add stripes to all the areas painted in lighter shades of green.

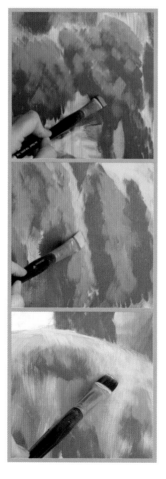

8 The crown of the tree is finished.

Tip
Create the effect of different distances through the changing shades of green. In this case, the farther away something is, the lighter the shade of green (through the addition of white) and the more blue you add.

9 With the mixture of colors from step 5 but in a buttery consistency, add detail to the trunk. Paint any visible branches in the same color.

10 Paint the dark reflections of any downward hanging branches with vertical brush strokes. Use a mixture of Prussian blue, light ocher, and a little vermilion.

Tip

Still water is usually painted with horizontal brush strokes, whereas vertical brush strokes are used for reflections. You can create a sense of movement by adding delicate diagonals with a fine brush.

11 Paint the lighter reflections with horizontal brush strokes. For these you need titanium white with a very little Prussian blue, and also pure titanium white.

12 The trunk, branches, and their reflections are now finished.

13 Finish painting the grass using chromium oxide green opaque, cadmium yellow light, a little titanium white, and a touch of vermilion. For the shadows under the trunk, mix Prussian blue and light ocher, with traces of titanium white, cadmium yellow light, vermilion and, as for all shadow colors, a hint of ultramarine.

14 Paint the trees at the sides in shades of very pale green and turquoise. Use the mixtures you already know for these, but with a larger proportion of blue and much more white. Finish their reflections in pale green and pale blue, by means of horizontal brush strokes. For the most distant background, add a little Prussian blue to titanium white and dab on with the brush.

15 Lastly, with fine strokes of the round brush, add detail to the structure of the lightest areas of foliage with titanium white, cadmium yellow light, and a pale blue mixed from chromium oxide green opaque, cadmium yellow light, titanium white, and Prussian blue.

16 After adding the highlights, give the background more structure by hinting at the trunks and branches of other trees. Add shadows to the far side of the lake.

SUMMARY

Dab in shades of green with a brush.

Trees at the side and in the background painted in less detail.

Fine stripes bring out the structure of the leaves.

Movement of the water shown by horizontal brush strokes.

Landscape

7

Our surroundings, the world in which we live, make a deep impression on us. We feel compelled to give artistic expression to the emotions they create within us by turning them into a picture and painting a landscape. "Landscape painting" means the depiction of scenery that may be the result of natural or human activity, or a mixture of both. The subject of a picture may be a natural landscape, but it could also be parkland, a townscape, an industrial landscape, or many other things.

FROM MINOR MATTER TO SUBJECT MATTER

Landscape painting, where the depiction of the world around us is an important subject, only really began in the late Middle Ages. Before that, the depiction of landscape in art was rarely of more than secondary importance. The only purpose of sketchily drawn buildings or countryside was to put the foreground figures in context.

It was only when people's view of nature changed—when the world was no longer the perishable stage through which they had to pass in order to achieve eternal happiness on the other side—that contemporary artists began to make an effort to capture and represent reality through accurate observation and view the landscape with a new, esthetic eye. Of course this also included attempting to depict the world in three dimensions and to capture the atmosphere and the particular phenomena produced by various times of day. Artists began to make systematic studies of different perspectives and developed their skills further through the use of brilliant color, subtle gradations of tone, and a new awareness of how best to use the effects of light and shade to create a sense of space, and to depict luminescent and atmospheric phenomena.

A lake scene *with interesting cloud formations.*

Figures and mythological stories were gradually sidelined, and the landscape became the actual subject of the picture—until the first purely landscape painting entirely without figures appeared some time around 1522. Of course architecture and figures continued to appear in landscape painting, and the landscape became the setting for mythological and historical scenes.

A WIDE RANGE

In the 17th century, when art made its way into the houses of the Dutch middle classes, there was a big demand for landscape paintings. The genre rapidly expanded into mountain, woodland, coastal, and river landscapes, fantasy and topographical landscapes, seascapes, winter landscapes, etc. These works were distinguished by their technical excellence in matters of tonal nuances, aerial perspective, and diverse effects of light. However, where matters of color selection are concerned, from time to time there was a vogue for monochrome paintings in blues, greens, and earth colors.

With the 19th century came a new trend in landscape painting. Lighter and brighter colors became increasingly important, while the interest moved from the subject to the method. The arrangement of forms and colors on the two-dimensional surface of the canvas became the focus of attention. The picture ceased to be a depiction of reality and became a reality in itself.

However, the painting of romantic landscapes intended to arouse emotions continued to flourish. With the advent of the Impressionists it became light and airy. They painted out of doors; the colors flowed into one another. The perception of things became more important than their meaning.

Interesting landscape with an idyllic village and a river in the background.

A morning landscape just after sunrise.

Monochrome landscape in shades of brown.

Archetypal landscape in the style of a postcard.

Special
Clouds

You rarely see a landscape without clouds. For one thing, cloudless days are a rarity, at least in temperate regions. And for another, a beautiful cloud formation is what makes a sky really interesting. The combination of clouds and the rays of a low sun always produces dramatic effects. From the point of view of composition, clouds can always be introduced into a painting in order to balance the distribution of the subject matter and add a little extra weight in a particular area. Clouds are a subject in their own right, and are always painted first when blocking in a sky.

COLOR, TECHNIQUE, FORMS

If you want to paint clouds in the best possible way, three considerations are particularly important:
1. The choice of colors
2. The correct brush strokes
3. Painting following the shapes.

For fair-weather clouds, paint the darker areas using a mixture of burnt sienna and ultramarine. For heavy rain clouds, use raw umber and Prussian blue. Of course you will need plenty of titanium white to make the tones lighter. Depending on the weather and the time of day, many other colors may be added, for instance yellow, orange, and violet.

Using a brush, you start by applying the dark colors, and then mix them with lots of titanium white, painting in semicircles and following the shapes of the clouds. This will produce the effect of a typical cumulus cloud.

The series of pictures on this double page is intended to show you how best to go about painting clouds.

1 After making a preliminary sketch, block in the clouds with burnt sienna, ultramarine, and titanium white, thinned with plenty of water. Be sure to follow the contours of the clouds with your brush right from the start.

2 The clouds have been blocked in first as the most important element in the picture.

3 Using the wet-into-wet technique (good for soft transitions), concentrate on one section of a cloud at a time. First apply a stripe of the dark color in a thick consistency, then a lot of titanium white on top, and mix the colors with semicircular movements of your brush.

4 If you still have a light-colored mixture on your brush, you can use it to start a new section of cloud and add the dark color afterward.

5 More distant clouds will be darker at the transition point with paler areas on top and at the front. To achieve this, dab paint on the darker areas of each cloud and work over them with titanium white.

6 Emphasize the light areas with increasing amounts of titanium white. Heightening the contrast between light and dark tones will make the clouds more three-dimensional.

7 Lastly, when the paint has dried, go over it once more with titanium white to bring the white areas even more into the foreground.

Dramatic sky

No two clouds are the same. An occasional look at the sky will confirm this. Anyone who takes up landscape painting will also have to press the clouds and their many different shapes into service. There are just 4 families of clouds, with 10 genera, 14 species, 9 subspecies, plus 9 special forms. As you can see, clouds are a real challenge for the painter, as well as making the sky a specific element of the picture requiring special attention.

Materials

Stretched canvas 24 x 32 inches (60 x 80 cm); household sponge; red chalk; flat brushes nos. 20 and 32; jar of water; cotton cloth or paper towels; palette; colors: vermilion, chrome yellow, titanium white, ultramarine, burnt sienna and crimson

Vermilion

Chrome yellow

Titanium white

Ultramarine

Burnt sienna

Crimson

1 Before you do the preliminary sketch, with the household sponge lay on a wash of very thin ultramarine. Sketch in the outlines of the clouds with red chalk, but don't spray with fixative.

2 Block in the clouds with mixtures of vermilion, chrome yellow, and titanium white, using semicircular brush movements.

3 Block in the dark areas in vermilion only, with slightly thicker paint and a fairly dry brush.

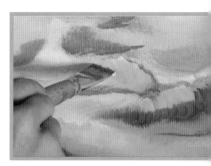

4 Emphasize the dark areas with a violet shade mixed from ultramarine and vermilion. The addition of titanium white produces a lighter shade.

5 The whole picture after step 4.

6 Emphasize the lightest areas with titanium white.

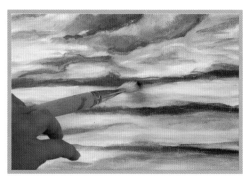

7 With the wash as your starting point, darken the lower half of the sky with ultramarine and a trace of burnt sienna.

8 Put in the detail of the dark clouds with a thick mixture of ultramarine and crimson.

9 The heightened contrast of dark and light creates an amazing sculptural effect.

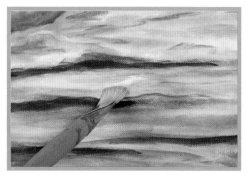

10 Using a dry brush with a thin mixture of titanium white, chrome yellow, a little vermilion, and a little burnt sienna, paint over selected areas of cloud to create a "smoky" effect.

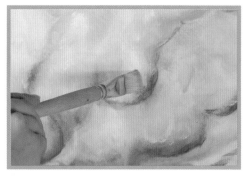

11 Paint the light areas with a mixture of titanium white and a little chrome yellow.

12 The painting is finished. The darkest areas have been emphasized with a mixture of ultra-marine and crimson.

SUMMARY

Orange tones for a dramatic evening sky.

"Smoky" effect after overpainting with a dry brush.

Rounded forms created by semicircular brush strokes.

Sculptural effect created by emphasizing the chiaroscuro.

Warm and cold

At one end of the rich spectrum of colors you have the warm colors. These are all the red shades, through orange to yellow and through red-violet and brown to ocher. The cold colors include all the blue shades through turquoise to green. In order to try out the different color ranges and gain experience, a good exercise is to paint the same (landscape) picture first in warm, then in cold colors. We will show you how to create it in warm colors and then compare it with the picture in cold colors.

Materials

Stretched canvas 24 x 32 inches (60 x 80 cm); pencil; flat brushes nos. 6, 14, and 20; jar of water; cotton cloth or paper towels; palette; colors: vermilion, dark madder, chrome yellow, and raw umber

 Vermilion

 Dark madder

 Chrome yellow

 Raw umber

1 Pencil in the contours of the landscape, paying particular attention to the details in the foreground.

2 Block in the field in the foreground in vermilion. Do not hesitate to apply the paint a little more thickly at this stage. Block in the fields in the middle and background in vermilion as well, but much more delicately.

3 Pick out the field edges, meadows, the shadowy side of the fence posts, and the road strongly in dark madder.

4 Paint the background fields in different strengths of dark madder thinned with water. Follow the structure of the fields with your brush strokes. Sketch in the most distant background (hills and sky) with very dilute dark madder.

5 Block in the sunlit sides with thin chrome yellow. In some places you will be painting over surfaces you have already painted.

6 In the background and foreground delicate shades of yellow will also appear.

7 Using raw umber, add the dark accents in the foreground. These include the shadowy areas on the fence posts, the paths between the fields, and the meadow grasses.

8 The farther away parts of the landscape are, the more you lighten and dilute the raw umber. Here it is best to use a dry brush.

9 Emphasize the red areas with another coat of vermilion, especially those in the foreground. Sketch a few clouds in the sky in vermilion.

10 Emphasizing the dark areas with raw umber and adding more vermilion has given the picture more depth.

11 Put in the final accents in dark madder.

Tip
Instead of using a ready-made brown, you can mix warm shades of red with a cool green to give a warm shade of brown.

LANDSCAPE IN COLD COLORS

However, you can also paint the same picture in cold colors. For this we used titanium white, cobalt blue, ultramarine, Prussian blue, chromium oxide green fiery, chromium oxide green opaque, and crimson. Although crimson actually belongs with the warm colors, it is used here to make a cool violet when mixed with a blue.

The cold colors create a wintery but nevertheless appealing mood.

12 View of Essenheim, using only warm colors.

View of Essenheim painted only in cold colors.

Irish landscape with lake

Ireland is rightly known as the Emerald Isle. This is chiefly due to the abundant rainfall. Before it flows out into the sea, the water collects in many small lakes, with occasional big tufts of grass protruding above the surface. An area of low pressure creating rapidly changing weather and skies plays its part in allowing us to create beautiful patterns in brief moments of bright sunlight against a background of gently rolling hills. Our picture was painted in southern Ireland at the Skellig ring in **County Kerry**.

Materials

Stretched canvas 24 x 28 inches (60 x 70 cm); red chalk; flat brushes nos. 12, and 18; jar of water; cotton cloth or paper towels; palette; colors: Prussian blue, light ocher, burnt sienna, titanium white, ultramarine, cadmium yellow light, and black

 Prussian blue

 Light ocher

 Burnt sienna

 Titanium white

 Ultramarine

 Cadmium yellow light

Black

1 The preliminary sketch in red chalk is not sprayed with fixative but partly painted into the first application of color. You should already pay attention to the structure of the grasses in the water and their correct proportions. Draw the contours in the foreground clearly; in the middle and background they should be increasingly unclear.

2 Block in the first layer of color for the water, the hills, and the sky in thin Prussian blue.

3 Use light ocher for the grasses, the edge of the bank, and part of the clouds. Mix a green from light ocher and Prussian blue, diluted with a lot of water. Use this to block in the water in front of the tufts of grass, the meadow on the left, and parts of the hills.

4 Use burnt sienna for the dark areas of the grasses and the shoreline.

5 Mix a gray from burnt sienna and Prussian blue, thinned and therefore made paler with a lot of water, and paint parts of the water, the hills, and the sky.

Tip

First set the line of the horizon in your landscape. Decide whether you want to give more importance to the scenery or the sky. Pictures that have the horizon in the middle often appear boring.

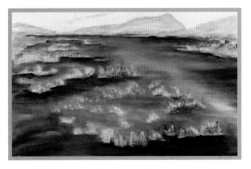

6 Add detail to the water by applying Prussian blue with horizontal brush strokes. Pick out the light patches with titanium white, which you will then overpaint with Prussian blue. Paint the detail of the grasses and the lake edge with burnt sienna and light ocher.

7 For the sky, use Prussian blue and titanium white applied side by side and painted into one another using horizontal brush strokes. For the clouds, use a mixture of burnt sienna and ultramarine, overpainted with a lot of titanium white.

8 Finish the mountains and landscape in a green mixed from cadmium yellow light, Prussian blue, and titanium white. Make the color stronger in the foreground and increasingly blue and pale in the background.

9 Paint the fine detail of the grasses in light ocher, burnt sienna, and titanium white. Detail the reflections in the water with Prussian blue, darkened with a little black.

10 Emphasize the darkest and lightest areas of the painting and add accents in cadmium yellow light, black, burnt sienna, and the green from step 3.

SUMMARY

Set the horizon.

Determine the structure and proportions of the grasses.

Aerial perspective: The mountains in the background become increasingly blue and pale.

Light patches on the water by brushing Prussian blue and titanium white together on the canvas.

Monochrome landscape

In a world full of color you can easily have too much of a good thing, so it's not surprising that there are artistic movements that concentrate on painting in a single color. There is no doubt that monochrome paintings have a particular appeal and a very special atmosphere. They look purist, simple, and beautiful. The landscape we show you here was painted using a single brown, plus the neutral colors white and black.

Materials

Stretched canvas 24 x 32 inches (60 x 80 cm); pencil; flat brushes nos. 12, 18, and 28; jar of water; cotton cloth or paper towels; palette; colors: Vandyke brown, titanium white, and black

  Vandyke brown

  Titanium white

  Black

1 Draw the outlines of the land-scape in pencil. At the same time, establish the horizon and note the perspective of the road and the trees and fence posts that get smaller toward the background.

2 Put Vandyke brown and black on your palette and paint the trees in brown and black. Omit the usual first application of paint and work with thick paint straight away.

3 The trees are finished.

4 Now it's the turn of the fence posts. Paint them in Vandyke brown and black, and add titanium white, so you can use your brush strokes to give them volume.

5 Paint the road wet-into-wet with thinner paint in all three colors.

6 Using the same technique as for step 5, but with much more titanium white, paint the meadow areas to the left and right of the road. Add in the shadows of the trees and fence posts.

7 Using all three colors, with Vandyke brown and black predominating, paint the grasses and bushes at the roadside.

8 Give emphasis to the darkest areas using black and the lightest with titanium white.

9 The sky has been painted pale and cloudless using a lot of titanium white—a little darker at the top and lighter toward the horizon. The line of the horizon has been slightly darkened.

SUMMARY

Paint applied impasto straight away.

Pale, cloudless sky using a lot of titanium white.

Main color Vandyke brown, using only white and black to lighten or darken it.

Perspective aided by rows of trees and fence posts.

8 Architecture

Architectural painting is concerned with the artistic treatment of buildings created by man, ranging from the simplest hut to the skyscraper. One of the reasons why buildings are so interesting is that, throughout the ages, the people who built them always tried to make them visually attractive as well as functional. Visitors to foreign cities and the artists who capture them with brush and paint find them equally fascinating. And subjects abound, often right outside your own front door.

PERSPECTIVE

Pictures, especially of buildings, only begin to look interesting when the painter has the skill to create an impression of space on the two-dimensional canvas, i.e. to depict three-dimensional objects in their correct perspective. The Ancient Greeks, and even more so the Romans, understood how to use perspective to represent three-dimensional space. After that, this skill fell into neglect for a time. Until the end of the Middle Ages, the dominant concept was perspective of importance, which meant that the size of the figures and objects depicted was determined by their importance in the picture, whereas their spatial relationship was of no significance. In the mid 15th century, at the time of the Renaissance, artists rediscovered perspective and developed it into central perspective as we know it.

Central perspective with one vanishing point.

VANISHING POINTS

Perspective is indispensable for the representation of three-dimensional space in a picture. All the imaginary or visible lines in the picture lead to one or more vanishing points. Central perspective is the simplest and most effective way of representing space. It has a single vanishing point, where all the lines leading into the depth of the space must meet. The picture you can see on this page has been created and painted in accordance with this principle.

If the standpoint of the viewer

moves from the center of a building or group of buildings to the side, a second vanishing point is created, because each set of horizontal lines at the sides of, for instance, a house, which are in reality parallel, runs to its own vanishing point at either side of the corner. As central perspective with a single perspective is also known as "one-point perspective," it is logical that this latter kind should be called "two-point perspective."

The picture of the bar on this page uses two vanishing points.

The horizontal lines of the building lead to two vanishing points.

THE BLACK SHOP BAR

beers   wines

No visible vanishing point, two dimensions.

PICTURE LAYOUT

Anyone responsible for the layout of a picture, whether photographer or painter, must always take perspective and vanishing points into consideration if they want to create eye-catching spatial effects. To put it another way: choosing the number and position of vanishing points are two of the essential tasks when designing a picture. This is because the vanishing points enable you to create a sense of movement and spatial depth. You can use them to add accents and bring objects into the line of vision.

One vanishing point

A street scene on the island of Mauritius is our starting point for discussion of the phenomenon of central perspective with a single vanishing point. All the lines leading back into space, which are in reality parallel, run together and meet at a point on the horizon that you have previously set at eye level. The crucial horizontals are the street and the buildings. The figures are also involved in the depiction of perspective.

Materials

Acrylic block 20 x 32 inches (50 x 64 cm); pencil; flat brushes nos. 12 and 18; round brushes sizes 4 and 8; jar of water; cotton cloth or paper towels; palette; colors: titanium white, black, ultramarine, cobalt blue, chrome yellow, light ocher, raw umber, vermilion

Titanium white

Black

Ultramarine

Cobalt blue

Chrome yellow

Light ocher

Raw umber

Vermilion

1 In the preliminary pencil drawing, fix your chosen vanishing points and get all the elements of the picture in perspective.

2 All the colors in this picture are painted thick from the start and applied side by side. Begin by painting the buildings and streets in mixtures of titanium white, black, and ultramarine blue.

3 Pay attention to the bright and shady sides. Paint the bright sides in shades right through to pure white, whereas the shady sides should become almost black.

4 With a mixture of chrome yellow, cobalt blue, and titanium white, paint things like the shutters and the balcony railings in a fresh turquoise.

5 For shady areas use a little less titanium white, adding a trace of ultramarine instead.

6 Paint parts of the buildings and streets and a few of the people using a mixture of titanium white, light ocher, and raw umber.

7 The sky and some parts of the buildings were painted with a mixture of ultramarine and cobalt blue, lightened with titanium white. For darker areas, add black to the mixture of blues.

8 Emphasize the dark accents with black. This includes both people and vehicles.

9 Using a dry brush, paint lines in black or with a mixture of light ocher and black.

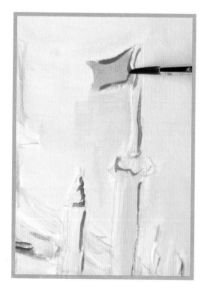

10 Where appropriate, use a mixture of light ocher and vermilion to add accents to the buildings.

11 Sketch in the faces and arms of the figures in light ocher. Add accents to their clothing with a mixture of light ocher and vermilion.

SUMMARY

Fix the horizon and vanishing points.

Get all the elements of the picture into perspective.

Darkest parts in the foreground, getting paler toward the background.

Apply the paint thickly from the start, with the colors side by side.

Two vanishing points

As soon as the viewer is no longer standing centrally in front of a building or group of buildings so that their walls are no longer parallel to him and he is looking at a corner, a second vanishing point is created (page 119). This example of a bar in Ireland, a kind of filling station for both people and vehicles, offers you a very good opportunity to practice perspective with two vanishing points. It is also interesting to note that—as with many paintings of single buildings—the vanishing points lie beyond the edge of the canvas.

Materials

Stretched canvas 12 x 12 inches (30 x 30 cm); pencil; flat brushes nos. 2, 6 and 10; jar of water; cotton cloth or paper towels; palette; colors: titanium white, ultramarine, cadmium yellow light, vermilion, Prussian blue, chromium oxide green fiery, dark madder, black

Titanium white

Ultramarine

Cadmium yellow light

Vermilion

Prussian blue

Chromium oxide green fiery

Dark madder

Black

1 In the preliminary pencil drawing, extend the lines leading to the vanishing points a little.

2 Mix a brown from ultramarine, cadmium yellow light, and vermilion. For the lighter parts of the house wall add titanium white and water. A little more ultramarine is needed for blocking in the shadows.

3 Block in the roof of the small neighboring hut to the right with vermilion. For the orange of the front, add a little cadmium yellow light, and for the shadow add ultramarine as before.

4 The first application of color has been completed. All the browns have been painted with the mixture from step 2. The wall of the neighboring house to the left was blocked in using a mixture of cadmium yellow light and titanium white, and the sky with very dilute ultramarine.

5 Add detail to the front wall of the house using a pale gray mixed from titanium white, a little Prussian blue, chromium oxide green fiery, and a little dark madder. For the shadows, add a little ultramarine.

6 Paint the barrel and the chair in the foreground in shades of gray. Use a little black as well for the darkest parts of the barrel.

7 Mix a dark brown from ultramarine, cadmium yellow light, vermilion and black and use this to paint the detail of the beams, the window frames, and the paintings on the wall of the house.

8 Paint the roof in shades of gray. Add a little ultramarine for the shady side. For the bright side of the chimney, add more titanium white.

9 For the signboards, use vermilion broken with a little ultramarine, plus spots of titanium white. The inn sign between the windows has been blocked in with a mixture of vermilion, cadmium yellow light, and titanium white.

11 Finish the detail of the neighboring house in shades of green, yellow, gray, and blue.

10 Complete the detail of the bar and the objects in front. Paint the writing on the sign above the door in gray and the pictures on either side of the text with dabs of different colors.

12 Add accents to the darkest and lightest spots.

13 The grays for the street were produced from the mixture in step 5, adding a little cadmium yellow light for the sidewalk close to the house. The sky has been finished using titanium white, ultramarine, and a very little Prussian blue.

SUMMARY

Emphasize the lightest and darkest areas.

Fix the horizon and the two vanishing points.

Heighten the sense of space through the use of light and shade.

Paint the objects in the foreground in detail.

Alley in Menton

Menton is a picturesque town in the South of France, or to be more precise, on the Côte d'Azur not far from the Italian border. It always pays to stroll through the narrow streets, sketchbook in hand, in search of suitable subjects. You can be lucky at any time. The preliminary study for this picture was done one lovely September afternoon. Of course, one-point perspective is also used in this painting.

Materials
Stretched canvas 28 x 20 inches (70 x 50 cm); round brush size 10; flat brushes nos. 22 and 18; jar of water; cotton cloth or paper towels; palette; colors: burnt sienna, chrome yellow, cobalt blue, raw umber, ultramarine, light ocher, and black

Burnt sienna

Chrome yellow

Cobalt blue

Raw umber

Ultramarine

Light ocher

Black

1 Make the preliminary sketch with a round brush and burnt sienna.

2 All the colors are applied transparent one after the other. Start with a green mixed from chrome yellow and cobalt blue, with a touch of burnt sienna.

3 Paint the shadow areas—the sun is coming from the left—in a gray mixed from raw umber and cobalt blue.

Tip

It is quite possible that the paint will run a little as you apply it. This does not matter, as long as it doesn't run too much, but be careful when adding water to the paint.

4 Paint the sunlit walls and steps in light ocher. Brush this color over the shadows as well.

5 Add accents to the darkest parts with black, applied more thickly. Mix in more water and emphasize the shadowy areas.

6 Emphasize the bright parts of the buildings with a mixture of chrome yellow and light ocher.

7 Paint the sky with a very dilute mixture of cobalt blue and ultramarine.

SUMMARY

Preliminary sketch using a round brush.

Colors applied transparent and in turn.

Pay attention to the perspective.

Light and shade heightens the sense of three-dimensionality.

Holiday memories

For many people, holidays are the times of the year they most look forward to. Every year we get the urge to leave home for a couple of weeks, either to head for distant shores or to see and experience something new in our own country. We are left with happy memories, which fortunately are quite slow to fade, especially if they have been captured in a picture. For people like you who have taken up painting, holiday memories are an ideal subject for a painting. You will be painting something you enjoy!

FROM ONE PICTURE TO ANOTHER

When people are away on holiday, they sometimes wish they had a kind of computer hard disk in their brain so they could store all the beautiful pictures they encounter every day and reproduce them at will—or better still print them out. It's a bit easier for people with camcorders or cameras, but even they can't capture everything. However, if you're a painter, you will carry your sketchbook with you all the time on holiday, and that gives you one advantage over all the optical and electronic gear. With a couple of strokes you can fix the image you still have in your head in your sketchbook in enough detail to be able to transfer it to canvas at your leisure.

From landscape to portrait format. *The photo of a sunset became the subject of a painting in an unusually tall, thin format.*

Sketched on the spot *and painted in watercolor, this bay on the Aegean coast of Turkey was painted in acrylics back home.*

Sunset

Is there anything more romantic than a sunset over the sea? Tastes differ, but the tourists who flock to west-facing shores every evening to enjoy this natural spectacle do not travel in vain. And if a fishing-boat happens to pass this way as well, the idyll is complete. You can see from the photo on page 131 that the subject of the picture we're about to paint really existed and is not merely the product of our imagination.

Materials
Stretched canvas 40 x 8 inches (100 x 20 cm); pencil; flat brushes nos. 2, 8, 12, 20, and 24; jar of water; cotton cloth or paper towels; palette; colors: cadmium yellow light, vermilion, dark madder, ultramarine, chromium oxide green fiery, Prussian blue, and titanium white

 Cadmium yellow light

 Vermilion

 Dark madder

 Ultramarine

 Chromium oxide green fiery

 Prussian blue

 Titanium white

1 The preliminary pencil drawing is kept very simple. All you need to do is sketch the outlines of the boat and the sun.

2 First block in the sun with cadmium yellow light in the upper part of the picture. Use vermilion for the lowest quarter circle. Where it is even darker, overpaint with a little dark madder. All these colors should be thinned with water.

3 Mix a dark gray from ultramarine, vermilion, and cadmium yellow light, and block in the boat.

4 Now we work from top to bottom. Block in the sky in a violet mixed from ultramarine and vermilion. Gradually add more blue as you get closer to the sun.

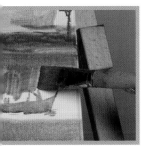

5 For blocking in the sea, add a little cobalt blue to the mixture from step 4, which will give a bluer shade of violet.

7 Finish painting the sun, first with cadmium yellow light, then with vermilion. Blur the colors wet-into-wet.

8 Add the dark accent to the setting sun in dark madder. Here again, blur the edges with a dry brush.

6 The first application is complete. The colors have run into one another a bit, but that is not a problem. After all, blocking is "only" the basis for the final painting.

133

9 To finish the boat, mix a classic black from chromium oxide green fiery, Prussian blue, and dark madder.

10 Using the mixture from step 4 but without adding water, finish the sky with regular, vertical brush strokes.

11 Finish the sea using the mixture from step 5 and horizontal brush strokes. Around the boat, use a narrower brush, still with horizontal brush strokes. Lighten the shade of blue with a little titanium white toward the foreground.

Tip
You can repeat the second coat on the sea and sky several times until you are satisfied with the result. Allow the paint to dry in between each coat.

12 Paint the dark patches and reflections in the water with the dark blue sea mixture and classic black respectively.

13 Emphasize the light spots delicately with titanium white.

14 Paint highlights on the boat with a mixture of cadmium yellow light and titanium white.

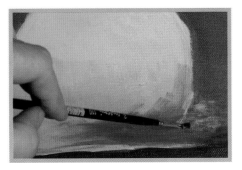

15 Add accents to the setting sun with cadmium yellow light, vermilion, and dark madder, sometimes slightly mixed.

16 Sparingly added highlights in titanium white heighten the romantic atmosphere. The orange shades of the sun are contrasted with the violet of the sky and the sea.

SUMMARY

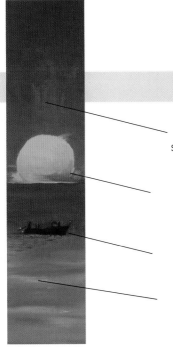

Gradually changing shades of violet in the sky.

Blur the red accents at the edges.

Boat in classic black.

Blue of the sea lightened with titanium white.

Boat

It is worth occasionally taking time to explore the areas close to your holiday resort on foot. The slower tempo will open your eyes to all kinds of interesting things to the left and right of the path. We were struck by this beached boat, which we came across along with a few others abandoned beside a bay. It seemed to be waiting for the moment when it would get back into the sea.

Materials

Stretched canvas 16 x 20 inches (40 x 50 cm); graphite stick; fixative; flat brushes nos. 6 and 20; jar of water, cotton cloth or paper towels; palette; colors: cobalt blue, light ocher, burnt sienna, titanium white, Prussian blue, chromium oxide green fiery, dark madder, cadmium yellow light, vermilion, and ultramarine

 Cobalt blue

 Light ocher

 Burnt sienna

 Titanium white

 Prussian blue

 Chromium oxide green fiery

 Dark madder

 Cadmium yellow light

 Vermilion

 Ultramarine

1 The preliminary sketch was completed using the grid method (pages 28 and 29). Use a graphite stick and spray with fixative until no more will wipe off.

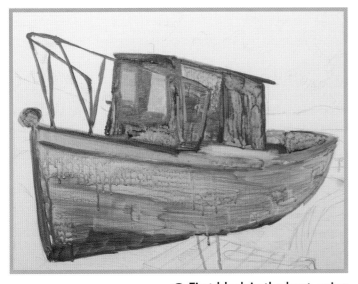

2 First block in the boat, using cobalt blue, light ocher, burnt sienna, and mixtures of these diluted with water.

3 Block in the boat and the crate in the right foreground in titanium white mixed with a very little chromium oxide green fiery, Prussian blue, and dark madder. Add more blue for the shady side.

4 Block in the hill in the background in light ocher and a mixture of light ocher and ultramarine.

5 The cliff in the right background has been blocked in with light ocher, ultramarine, and a little dark madder. For the sea, we used a mixture of Pruss- ian blue and titanium white. The ground in front of the boat and to the right is mainly burnt sienna mixed with ultramarine.

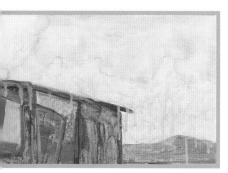

6 Block in the sky with cobalt blue mixed with ultramarine and thinned with a lot of water. For the clouds, use burnt sienna mixed with ultramarine and a lot of water.

7 Paint the wheelhouse of the boat in burnt sienna mixed with a little cobalt blue. For the darker areas add more blue, and for lighter parts mix in titanium white.

8 Finish the darkest parts of the inside of the stern with a mixture of Prussian blue, and burnt sienna. Add titanium white for the decking to its left. The board in the sun has been painted with pure titanium white.

9 For the forward part of the hull, mix titanium white with a little Prussian blue; for the after part use titanium white, light ocher, and burnt sienna. Blend the two mixtures in the middle. Follow the line of each plank with your brush strokes. Paint the darkest parts of the upper edge of the boat in burnt sienna mixed with a little Prussian blue and the darkest parts of the hull in cobalt blue, light ocher, and a little titanium white.

10 Mix a classic black from Prussian blue, chromium oxide green fiery, and dark madder to paint the darkest patches underneath the boat.

12 Paint the railings in burnt sienna.

13 Add highlights in titanium white.

11 Finish the background using the same color mixtures as for steps 4, 5, and 6, but in a buttery consistency and adding titanium white for the sky and clouds. Add more detail to the hull, the crate, and the upturned dinghy.

14 The grass around the boat has been painted in various shades of green, mixed from cadmium yellow light, ultramarine, and a touch of vermilion, sometimes lightened with titanium white.

SUMMARY

Brush strokes following the planks.

Light and shade emphasize three-dimensionality.

Darkest areas in classic black.

Add highlights in titanium white.

Aegean bay

Why do we humans always feel drawn to the sea and the shore? Even lovers of the countryside and mountains sometimes feel at home there. Is it because all our distant ancestors came from the sea? Whatever the reason, a picturesque spot beside a bay always delights the eye. Artists especially should linger a while to soak in its beauty and to keep the memory alive by first sketching it and then capturing it on canvas with paint and brush.

Materials

Stretched canvas 20 x 28 inches (50 x 70 cm); pencil; fixative; flat brushes nos. 6, 10, and 28; jar of water, cotton cloth or paper towels; palette; colors: light ocher, burnt sienna, Prussian blue, cadmium yellow light, chromium oxide green fiery, vermilion, cobalt blue, and titanium white

Light ocher

Burnt sienna

Prussian blue

Cadmium yellow light

Chromium oxide green fiery

Vermilion

Cobalt blue

Titanium white

1 The preliminary drawing in pencil includes all the essential elements. The columns framing the bay are particularly eye-catching.

2 The first blocking in has been done with light ocher, burnt sienna, Prussian blue, and mixtures of these three colors, all thinned with plenty of water. Broadly speaking, they represent the primary colors yellow, red, and blue.

3 The first application of paint has been completed. The shadows are already blocked in, whereas the stone paving is painted in only two dimensions.

4 Next put in the detail of the columns, using a mixture of light ocher and Prussian blue for the shady side. For the light areas, mix light ocher and titanium white. Your brush strokes should follow the structure of the columns.

5 Work on the paving stones with the same mixtures as for the columns, using horizontal brush strokes. For the cracks between them, add burnt sienna. Your brush strokes should follow the direction of the cracks.

6 Mix burnt sienna and Prussian blue and paint the darkest parts of the tree on the left. Add titanium white for the lighter parts. Follow the structure of the bark with your brush.

7 Greens! For the leaves of this tree, mix all kinds of greens, for example from light ocher and cobalt blue, and dab the colors on side by side. Use titanium white to lighten the various mixtures.

8 The foreground is complete, apart from the tree on the right.

9 You can make paler shades of green, for instance using cadmium yellow light and cobalt blue. Finish the tree on the right with these, dabbing the paint on with your brush.

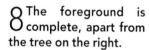

10 Paint the town beside the bay with dabs of many different colors. Use light ocher, titanium white, vermilion, and a gray mixed from Prussian blue, burnt sienna, and titanium white.

11 The sea has been finished with a mixture of Prussian blue, cobalt blue, a very little chromium oxide green fiery, and titanium white. The mountains are painted in shades of green, getting blue and paler into the distance.

12 Add the lightest spots—here the crests of a few waves—in titanium white.

13 The sky has been finished using a mixture of Prussian blue, cobalt blue, and titanium white. It gets paler toward the horizon, turning almost to a pale orange mixed from titanium white with a little vermilion and light ocher. Show the sky shining through the trees to left and right with spots of pale blue.

SUMMARY

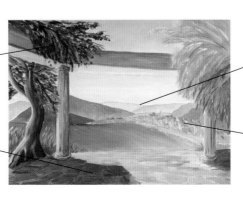

Leaves of the left-hand tree in various shades of dark green.

Light and shade on the tree and the ground create three-dimensionality.

Aerial perspective with sky and mountains paler closer to the horizon.

Town sketched in with dabs of color.

Figures

10

Portraying figures in their correct proportions is certainly not one of the easiest tasks in painting so, if you are to succeed, it is essential to have a basic grasp of human anatomy and some experience of drawing. The be all and end all of good figure drawing is keeping to the **correct proportions, because if any part ends up too big or too small, it quickly destroys the good effect. This means you will have to practice long and hard in order to achieve the precision needed for this genre.**

PROPORTION AND RULES

The proportions must be correct. This is easily said, but how can success be achieved? People have been pondering the question of correct proportions for centuries. Leonardo da Vinci's drawing of "Vitruvian Man," showing a man with arms and legs outstretched in various positions framed in a circle and a square, is well known. Incidentally, Vitruvius was a Roman architect who developed a set of compulsory rules or instructions for designing columns, on which the proportions of the other parts of the building were based.

In fine art, and therefore in painting, the rules constitute a method for relating the proportions of one part of the human body to another, based on a unit of measurement. This unit is the human head.

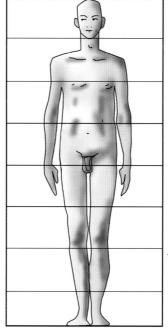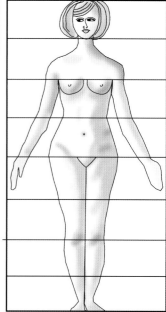

The rules for the human body of a man and a woman. It is divided into eight zones, each section corresponding to the size of the head measured from the crown to the chin.

Tip
Before and while practicing, you should keep looking at photos or successful paintings of people in different positions in order to gain an understanding of the proportions of individual parts of the body.

The proportions vary with changes *in the position of the joints, depending on the angle of particular parts of the body to the viewer.*

FROM TOP TO TOE

Unfortunately, in figure studies it all too often happens that the head ends up much too large in relation to the rest of the body. This is reason enough to make it the unit of measurement for keeping the proportions correct. The procedure is as follows: The human body is divided from top to bottom into eight equal sections. The height of each section corresponds to the length of the head from the crown to the chin. This means that the following seven regions of the body are to be painted in the same proportion as the head:

1. from the chin to the nipples
2. from the nipples to the waist
3. from the waist to the pubic bone
4. from the pubic bone to the thigh
5. from the thigh to the bend of the knee/top of the shin
6. from the bend of the knee/top of the shin to the calf
7. from the calf to the sole of the foot.

Obviously people vary and individual differences may occur. In addition, the average ratio of upper body to lower body for women is 1:1, whereas for men the upper body is relatively shorter in relation to the lower body. Nevertheless, these rules provide a useful guideline, which you will benefit from following.

Incidentally, the proportions for children should not be determined by this method. Small children have a ratio of 5.5:1 (at 1 unit, the head is distinctly bigger than the rest of the body). For a child aged about 10, the correct ratio is 6.5:1.

SHORTER WHEN SEATED

As soon as a person is no longer standing upright, for instance when they go to sit down, the proportions of individual parts of the body as represented will change. This is due first and foremost to a change of perspective, which in turn depends on the position of the viewer. Some parts of the body appear longer, others shorter than before, and a bent back no longer appears the same length as it does when standing straight.

Four friends

Observing the principle of starting with something easy and progressing to the more difficult, as an introduction to the genre of figure-painting we have chosen a subject that is really easy to paint. The starting point was a photo of four men walking toward the horizon on a bright, sunny day. Only their slender silhouettes can be made out in the shimmering heat. Though it is not a matter of portraying figures in detail, the proportions must nevertheless be correct.

Materials

Stretched canvas 20 x 28 inches (50 x 70 cm); graphite stick; flat brushes nos. 6 and 18; jar of water; cotton cloth or paper towels; palette; colors: burnt sienna, raw umber, black, titanium white, light ocher, cobalt blue, and ultramarine

Burnt sienna

Raw umber

Black

Titanium white Cobalt blue

Light ocher Ultramarine

1 In the preliminary drawing with graphite stick, which you don't spray with fixative, first set the line of the horizon. Draw only very simplified figures.

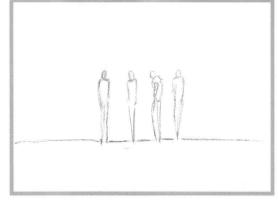

2 Using the paint opaque from the start, paint the people with mixtures of burnt sienna, raw umber, and black, giving the bodies different tonal values.

3 Paint the ground with mixtures of titanium white, light ocher, and raw umber. Paint over the graphite line of the horizon.

4 How attractive the ground looks will be determined by the variety of shades you create by blending the various color mixtures on the canvas.

5 For the sky, mix cobalt blue and ultramarine with just a touch of black. Lighten with increasing amounts of titanium white as you get closer to the horizon. Break the blue with a little raw umber close to the horizon.

6 Paint the outlines and bodies of the figures in the same colors as in step 2, but with a little more black.

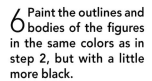

7 A lovely picture has been created using simple means—and you have familiarized yourself with the genre of figure painting.

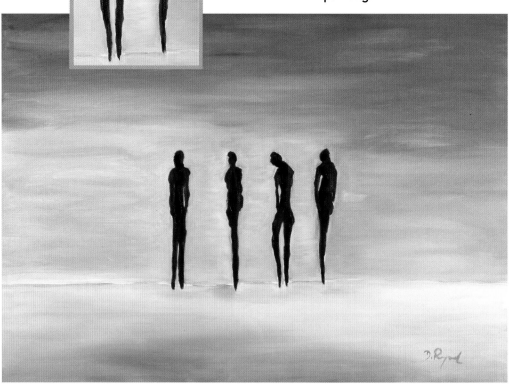

SUMMARY

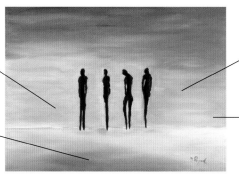

Sky becoming lighter toward the horizon.

Figures in shades of brown and black.

Paint the ground in different shades.

Brown shades in the sky near the line of the horizon.

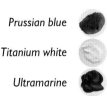

African

After the four friends pausing on the way to the horizon, this man from Africa is the subject for our next figure painting. This is a more challenging task, because this person is not standing but sitting on a ledge in a room. As a result, some of the proportions of the body will be different in the painting. However, the lines here are still clear and the proportions recognizable. Only the torso and the lower legs need to be adjusted for perspective.

Materials

Stretched canvas 24 x 28 inches (60 x 70 cm); pencil; graphite stick; fixative; flat brushes nos. 8 and 20; jar of water; cotton cloth or paper towels; palette; colors: light ocher, burnt sienna, vermilion, black, Prussian blue, titanium white, and ultramarine

Light ocher		Prussian blue	
Burnt sienna		Titanium white	
Vermilion		Ultramarine	
Black			

1 In the preliminary sketch, first draw the figure in pencil and the shadow in graphite stick and spray with fixative, and only then draw the room. Pay attention to the shapes and volumes of the human body.

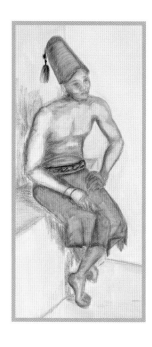

2 Using burnt sienna thinned with water, block in the skin tones. Use burnt sienna mixed with vermilion for the clothing, and light ocher and black for the belt.

3 Use light ocher thinned with water for the first application of color for the room. Add the details of light and shade to the body surfaces using burnt sienna, light ocher, Prussian blue, black, and titanium white.

4 Finish the clothing in vermilion, darkened with black in places, and the belt with light ocher, black, and titanium white.

5 Paint the shadows in a mixture of light ocher, burnt sienna, and a little ultramarine. For the floor and walls, use various shades made from light ocher, burnt sienna, and titanium white.

6 Put in the deepest shadows on the body and emphasize the light spots. Do the same for the clothing and jewelry.

7 The background and the shadows have been worked over one more time.

SUMMARY

Light and shade heighten the sense of space.

Add highlights in titanium white.

Pay attention to the folds in the clothing.

Portray the anatomy and proportions correctly.

Market scene

Depicting people in their own surroundings is a subdivision of figure painting. It is known as genre painting, which means the painting of scenes of everyday life that come from the artist's own times and sur-roundings. This picture is based on a sketch (page 30) that was made in a weekly market in Turkey. In our description, we will be concentrating primarily on how the figures are developed.

Materials
Stretched canvas 20 x 24 inches (50 x 60 cm); pencil; fixative; flat brushes nos. 2, 6, 18, and 32; jar of water; cotton cloth or paper towels; palette; colors: light ocher, ultramarine, burnt sienna, raw umber, chrome yellow, vermilion, chromium oxide green fiery, black, titanium white, and cobalt blue

 Light ocher

 Ultramarine

 Burnt sienna

 Raw umber

 Chrome yellow

 Vermilion

 Chromium oxide green fiery

 Black

 Titanium white

 Cobalt blue

1 Do the preliminary pencil drawing corresponding to the sketch. Make the foreground very detailed, the middle and background sketchy. Cover with a wash of light ocher thinned with a lot of water.

2 After the wash, use the paint opaque straight away. The skin tones of the foreground figures are mixed from burnt sienna, raw umber, and a little ultramarine, lightened with titanium white.

3 On the market stall in the foreground, the bottles were painted in light ocher, ultramarine, and titanium white, and the cans in burnt sienna, raw umber, and vermilion.

4 Paint the sun umbrella with mixtures of chromium oxide green fiery, chrome yellow, and ultramarine. For the cold box use cobalt blue and titanium white.

5 The ground has been painted in raw umber, titanium white, and black, using horizontal brush strokes.

6 Paint the figures, stalls, and umbrellas in the background with burnt sienna, cobalt blue, vermilion, chromium oxide green fiery, chrome yellow, and black.

7 Using mixtures of burnt sienna, black, and lots of titanium white, paint the houses. Merely indicate the windows and doors in black, using a fine brush.

8 Using a fairly fine brush, paint the details of the figures. This includes the shades of the clothing, here finished in titanium white, black, and ultramarine.

9 Detail the facial expressions—no easy task— and darken the shadowy side of the figures with raw umber and a little ultramarine.

10 Add light and shade to the traders' wares, which will make the painting more three-dimensional.

12 Now paint the background in more precise and careful detail. For example, you could darken the shadows on the ground a little with raw umber, black, and titanium white.

11 Paint the sky in ultramarine, cobalt blue and titanium white. Darken the shadows on the ground with raw umber, black, and titanium white—dark in the foreground and getting lighter toward the background.

13 The last details in the foreground, middle ground, and background have been brought out. This traditionally includes adding highlights and emphasizing the darkest areas.

SUMMARY

Umbrella in foreground finely detailed.

Hint at the windows and doors of the houses.

Bring out the light and shade on the market stall.

Figures carefully painted in detail.

Animals

Animals are our best friends—not everyone loves them all, but each to their own taste. And we enjoy painting the things that please and fascinate us. Painting animals is similar to painting people. Only accurate knowledge of the anatomy of the species in question, plus plenty of experience in drawing animals will produce top quality results. So pick up your pencil and start by drawing living creatures in your sketchbook.

DOG, CAT, MOUSE

What makes animals more difficult to paint than humans is the fact that there are so many different species. Two, four, six, eight or more legs, with or without wings—and with a huge variety of body shapes.

You probably have one or more favorites that you would most like to devote yourself to. Once again, accuracy is required when it's a matter of getting the proportions right. You should know the measurements and the play of light and shade as well as the structure of the skin, fur, plumage etc.

***Dogs and cats** are the most popular pets—and definitely the favorite subjects when it comes to painting animals.*

***Horses are elegant, powerful, and hardworking** —and especially popular with young girls.*

Cat

Details are important in our first animal painting. The cat's face in particular requires meticulous work with fine brushes, and the preliminary drawing should, of course, provide an adequate basis. Especial care should be taken with the eyes. The size of the head and upper body must be in the correct proportion to one another. The drawing and structure of the fur show you the appropriate direction for the brush strokes.

Materials
Beechwood block 8 x 12 inches (20 x 30 cm); masking tape; white wall paint; pencil; flat brushes nos. 2, 6, and 20; jar of water; cotton cloth or paper towels; palette; colors: titanium white, raw umber, light ocher, black, cadmium yellow light, vermilion, and ultramarine

Titanium white

Raw umber

Light ocher

Black

Cadmium yellow light

Vermilion

Ultramarine

1 Tape over the parts of the block that are not to be painted. Then prime the wood as described on page 17. Make a detailed preliminary drawing in pencil.

2 Apply the colors opaque. Paint the darkest parts of the cat's head with a mixture of raw umber and black.

3 For the paler parts, add traces of light ocher and vermilion and lighten with titanium white. Paint the very lightest parts in titanium white with pale blue patches in between, mixed from titanium white and a little ultramarine.

4 After putting in the nose in a pink mixed from titanium white, a little vermilion, and light ocher, paint round the edges of the eyes with a mixture of raw umber and black. Paint the irises with a mixture of ultramarine and black. At the bottom, paint a pale blue curve with a mixture of titanium white and a little ultramarine. Use black for the pupils, and titanium white for the lightest reflections in the eyes.

5 Mix the color for the dark brown patches of fur from raw umber and a little light ocher, vermilion, and titanium white. For the lighter brown fur add more titanium white.

6 Paint the pale fur with titanium white and the pale blue from step 3.

7 The painting of the cat itself has been completed.

8 Paint the plants on the left in various shades of green mixed from ultramarine, cadmium yellow light, and titanium white, occasionally adding a little vermilion.

Advice

Do not fail to prime the wood. If it is not primed, the paints will sink in too far and go dull, whereas if the wood is primed, they will shine out brilliantly.

9 Use titanium white mixed with ultramarine, raw umber, and a little cadmium yellow light for the light background on the right-hand side of the picture.

10 Paint the dark background above the cat with a mixture of raw umber and ultramarine, slightly lightened with titanium white. Finish the edge of the cat's fur by picking up a little of the raw umber and titanium white mixture on a dry brush and applying it carefully.

11 With a dry brush, pick up a very small amount of titanium white and paint a few short, smooth strokes over the background for the cat's whiskers.

12 All the paint has been applied. Now pull off the masking tape.

13 When the picture is dry, you can apply a coat of varnish.

SUMMARY

Paint the fur following its structure.

Use pale blue in the fur to make the cat more three-dimensional.

Eyes in various shades of ultramarine.

Pupils in black, reflections in the eyes in titanium white.

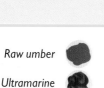

Step by step
Three elephants

Of all Africa's wild animals, elephants are the most impressive giants among the so-called "big five." If they happen to appear against the background of a dramatic landscape, the beauty of the scene is almost perfect. Of course in our latitudes it is extremely unlikely that a herd of elephants will cross your path, but photos from books and newspapers or a visit to the zoo are perfectly good when it comes to finding a model.

Materials
Acrylic block 20 x 25 inches (50 x 64 cm); pencil; flat brushes nos. 10 and 18; jar of water; cotton cloth or paper towels; palette; colors: raw umber, ultramarine, vermilion, titanium white, light ocher, cadmium yellow light, crimson, and black

Raw umber

Ultramarine

Vermilion

Titanium white

Light ocher — Crimson

Cadmium yellow light — Black

1 In the preliminary pencil drawing, fix the horizontal line between the plain and the mountain. Draw the outlines of the elephants, indicating the shadows and volume.

2 Block in the elephants in a gray mixed from raw umber, ultramarine, and a little vermilion. Lighten the gray with titanium white in various places.

3 Using mixtures of light ocher, ultramarine, and titanium white, block in the ground and parts of the mountain. You should already be paying attention to light and shade.

4 Block in the mountain, trees, and some of the shadow areas with a mixture of raw umber, ultramarine, light ocher, and a little vermilion.

5 Finish the ground in the same colors as for step 3, but add cadmium yellow light to the mixtures.

Tip

When applying the second coat, you don't have to paint completely over all areas. A picture also gets life from surfaces that were painted earlier shining through.

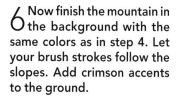 Now finish the mountain in the background with the same colors as in step 4. Let your brush strokes follow the slopes. Add crimson accents to the ground.

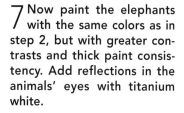 Now paint the elephants with the same colors as in step 2, but with greater contrasts and thick paint consistency. Add reflections in the animals' eyes with titanium white.

8 Finish the detail of the ground and the mountain, using the same colors as in steps 3 and 4. Emphasize individual tufts of grass and trees.

9 Put in the last accents in the darkest areas in black. Emphasize the light spots with titanium white.

SUMMARY

Set the horizon between the plain and the mountain.

Follow the slope of the mountain with your brush strokes.

Paint the elephants in various shades of gray.

Emphasize the grasses in many places.

Stretched canvases

12

Stretched canvases are the most popular of all the supports we have described in this book. You can buy prestretched canvases in various shapes and sizes, paint on them straight away, and hang your finished work on the wall without going to very much trouble. Even without a frame, the painting looks valuable and attractive. The painting surface, usually made of cotton or linen, is already primed and needs no additional treatment, so you can start enjoying the pleasures of painting immediately.

BEFORE AND AFTER BUYING

When purchasing prestretched canvases, check that the painting surface is undamaged and the stretcher isn't warped. The primed fabric should have no dents and the angles at the corners must match. We recommend stretchers where the canvas is fastened at the back. Check the package to see that all the wedges supplied—usually eight—have been included.

After purchase and before painting on the canvas, put the wedges in place as shown on this page, with the points in the grooves provided, and hammer them in a little way.

Hammer the wedges *a little way into the grooves.*

If there are any dents *in the canvas, rub gently with a wet household sponge.*

Advice
If you failed to spot a dent in the primed canvas when you bought it, this can easily be remedied by sprinkling the back of the spot with a little water and rubbing gently with a household sponge. The fabric will contract again as it dries, and the dent will disappear.

HANGING STRETCHED CANVASES

"That picture's not hanging straight!" is a frequently heard comment that can easily be prevented. With the right technique and equipment you will have no trouble showing your work in a professional manner. We recommend using wire and screw eyes for hanging, because it is stable and simple—all you need is a hook on the wall.

1 Fix the screw eyes in the upper third of the stretcher but, even in the case of large-format paintings, no more than 8 inches (20 cm) from the top edge. Measure to be sure the two hanging points are at the same height and screw the eyes into the wood.

2 Pull the picture wire through the eye, make a loop, and wind the short end round the long end several times.

3 To hang heavier pictures, secure the wire additionally with a crimp sleeve.

COMPOSITIONS USING STRETCHED CANVASES

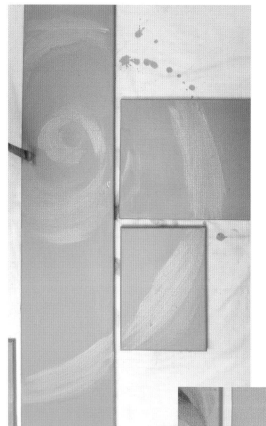

Not only are stretched canvases practical and attractive to paint on, they can also be used in combination as elements in a composition. You can assemble a mosaic of different sizes and formats, distributing your painting across all the canvases, and then hang them that way on the wall. This double-page spread shows a composition made up of four canvases.

ORANGE, YELLOW, RED

First the surfaces and sides of all the canvases were painted with an orange mixed from a lot of primary yellow, cadmium yellow light, and a little vermilion. This was repeated after the first application had dried.

After positioning the canvases on the floor in the arrangement in which they would later hang, the parts were painted with energetic sweeps of the brush, first with cadmium yellow light, then with vermilion, and finally with crimson. The most important thing was to paint over all four canvases at once with big, almost uninterrupted, sweeping movements. Dry patches at the edges were painted in orange again and smeared while wet with the yellow and red shades.

After the first coat of orange, *paint over all canvases in great sweeps of cadmium yellow light.*

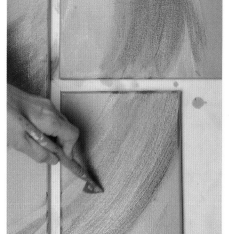

Next come great sweeps *of vermilion and*

Materials

Four stretched canvases: 40 x 8 inches (100 x 20 cm), 9 x 12 inches (24 x 30 cm), and two 7 x 9 inches (18 x 24 cm); flat brushes nos. 32 and 20; jar of water; cotton cloth or paper towels; palette; colors: primary yellow, cadmium yellow light, vermilion, and crimson

Primary yellow

Cadmium yellow light

Vermilion

Crimson

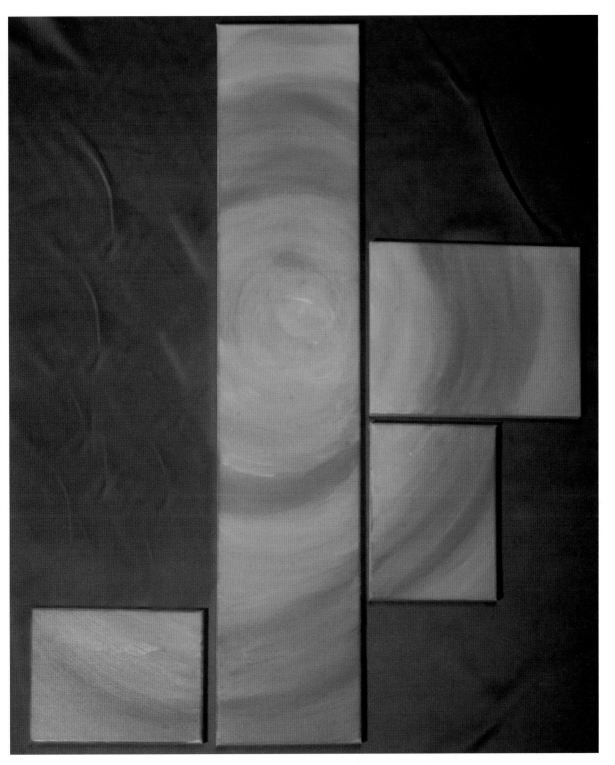

The finished work, *shown on a blue ground.*

Step by step
Cluster of shells

In addition to triangles, rectangles, squares, and hexagons, stretched canvases also come in special shapes that are ideal for attractive creations. For you, we have chosen a square canvas with a gap in the middle. In addition to paint, we also used filler, acrylic gel, and various objects that we introduced into the picture. The result is known as an "assemblage," i.e. the combining of various random objects into a three-dimensional work of art.

Materials

Stretched canvas: 24 x 24 inches (60 x 60 cm), with a square gap; pencil; palette knife; flat brushes nos. 12 and 16; jar of water; cotton cloth or paper towels; coarse filler; fine filler; palette; colors: titanium white, Vandyke brown, light ocher, ultramarine, Prussian blue, and chromium oxide green fiery; cord; wood glue; thick acrylic gel; small pebbles; shells

Titanium white

Vandyke brown

Light ocher

Ultramarine

Prussian blue

Chromium oxide green fiery

1 After marking a square round the edge of the gap in pencil, fill this area with coarse filler.

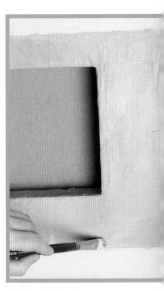

2 Spread fine filler over the remainder of the surface with flowing hand movements. Allow both types of filler to dry.

3 Paint the inner square with a mixture of Vandyke brown and light ocher, lightened with a lot of titanium white.

4 Paint the outer area and the outside edges with a mixture of ultramarine, Prussian blue, and chromium oxide green fiery, also lightened with a lot of titanium white.

5 Wind a thick cord several times round the left-hand side of the frame. Fasten the ends at the back with wood glue.

6 Now, using a palette knife, apply very thick acrylic gel that will be transparent when dry. Work from top to bottom, tapering off toward the cord.

7 Cover the freshly applied acrylic gel with tiny stones, pushing them gently into the gel with your hand.

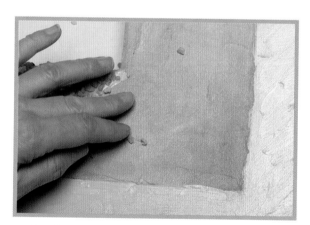

8 Single stones around the edges, also attached with acrylic gel, complete the design.

9 Now it's time for the shells. Distribute them where they look best and attach them with acrylic gel as for the stones.

10 The "shell cluster" is finished—an abstract picture with a maritime look. The colors and materials are in perfect harmony, conveying the desired atmosphere.

SUMMARY

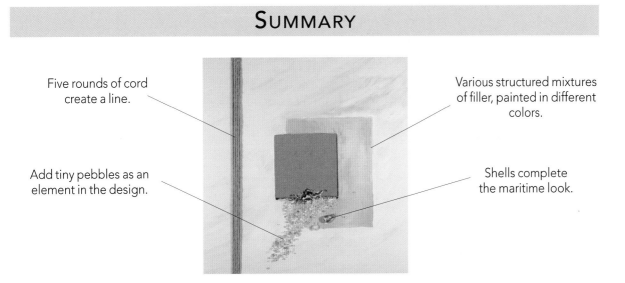

Five rounds of cord create a line.

Various structured mixtures of filler, painted in different colors.

Add tiny pebbles as an element in the design.

Shells complete the maritime look.

Experiments

In the picture "Cluster of Shells" on the preceding pages we have already abandoned the world of representational painting on a two-dimensional ground. In addition to the painted image, objects were added to the work and arranged as part of the composition, opening the way to a true third dimension. The materials used here basically set no limits to trial and experimentation. Finding suitable materials gets easier each time, as you become more involved in it.

FINDS

In the early 20th century, artists began to work two-dimensional objects such as newspaper cuttings, pages from books, sheets of music etc. into their paintings. This form of artistic expression is known as collage. When three-dimensional objects are added or used exclusively as elements in the picture, it is known as an "assemblage."

Adding all kinds of finds—to suit every different taste—is still popular and produces attractive results. This page shows you a few typical finds we collected by the wayside, but you can also buy similar things or use things that have accumulated in your own home.

Leaf, bark, horse chestnuts, and golden fabric.

Shells are among the most popular things to find and collect.

Wall object

The finale to our brief excursion into experimental painting with acrylics is a second assemblage. The ground consists of two differently shaped wooden frames, which are combined to form a single object. In it we have placed things we have found in the countryside. Once again the effort expended—apart from the arrangement—is small, but the resulting effect is even greater. With the right lighting, you can enhance the spatial effect after the object has been hung.

Materials

Square beechwood painting block 16 x 16 inches (40 x 40 cm); triangular beechwood block with 12 inch (30 cm) sides; white wall paint; flat brush no. 20; jar of water; cotton cloth or paper towels; coarse filler; fine filler; palette; colors: crimson and dark madder; stones; tree bark; wood glue

Crimson

Dark madder

1 Prime the wood blocks with white paint (page 17). Arrange the individual elements of your object and assemble it all on a horizontal surface. Consider the best way to distribute sizes and quantities, and mark the positions in pencil.

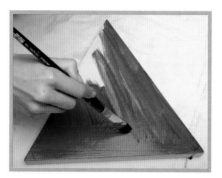

2 Disassemble the objects again and paint the square block in crimson and the triangle in dark madder. Repeat this coat if necessary. The marking will still be visible to start with.

3 When the paint has dried, first stick the triangle to the square where previously arranged and marked with wood glue. Then glue on the pieces of bark.

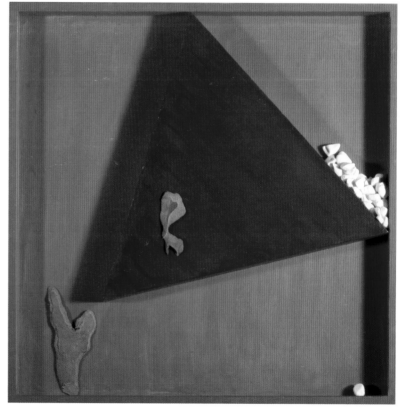

4 When the glue has dried, put the frame of the object upright and glue on the stones.

5 The object is finished and ready to be presented.